The Maker and the Myth:
Faulkner and Yoknapatawpha,
1977

The Maker and The Myth:

FAULKNER AND YOKNAPATAWPHA,
1977

EDITED BY
EVANS HARRINGTON
AND
ANN J. ABADIE

UNIVERSITY PRESS OF MISSISSIPPI
JACKSON · 1978

Manufactured in the United States of America
Designed by J. Barney McKee

This volume is authorized & sponsored by the
University of Mississippi
University, Mississippi

Library of Congress Cataloging in Publication Data
  Main entry under the title:

  The Maker and the Myth.

  Papers presented at a conference held at the University of
Mississippi in 1977.
  Includes bibliographical references.
  1. Faulkner, William, 1897-1962—Congresses.
2. Southern States in literature—Congresses.
I. Harrington, Evans. II. Abadie, Ann J.
PS3511.A86Z489 1977   813'.5'2   78-60158
ISBN 0-87805-049-3
ISBN 0-87805-075-2 pbk.

PS
3511
.A86
Z489
1977

Contents

Introduction

The essays in this volume were originally presented as lectures at the Fourth Annual Faulkner and Yoknapatawpha Conference held on the Oxford campus of the University of Mississippi July 31 through August 5, 1977. In "Faulkner's Localism" Calvin S. Brown shows how the Nobel Prize winner used details from Lafayette County, his "little postage stamp of native soil," to make his Yoknapatawpha myth. In describing the "intense localism" of Faulkner's settings, characters, language, and traditions, Brown draws on his research for *A Glossary of Faulkner's South* and on personal knowledge: he was a younger contemporary of William Faulkner in Oxford for many years, and his boyhood home on the University campus was located about a hundred yards from the house in which the first four Yoknapatawpha novels were written. For his second essay, "Faulkner's Universality," Brown draws on his lifelong study and teaching of comparative literature. After discussing the "naively ingenious myth-hunting" of many critics, Brown concludes that Faulkner's parallels with the great myths are due to his universality, a quality which is characterized by his fondness for aphorisms, his devotion to even-handed justice, his reflection of universally accepted human observations and values, his presentation of characters who are recognizable types, and his use of universal themes.

History and myth are large topics brilliantly explored by Lewis P. Simpson in two essays, "Sex and History: Origins of

Introduction

Faulkner's Apocrypha" and "Yoknapatawpha and Faulkner's Fable of Civilization." In the first essay Simpson surveys Faulkner's pre-Yoknapatawpha fiction and his developing understanding of the cosmological and historical modes of consciousness. In *Flags in the Dust*, Simpson writes, Faulkner perceived "a crisis in sexuality" and discovered "in the history of the South a singular yet compelling representative exemplification of this crisis." Simpson then shows how the Yoknapatawpha novels are "a great, ironic, often enigmatic testament to the capacity of the literary imagination to conceive the drama of the historical consciousness in its formation and in its completion and to conceive this as a tale told by the modern literary artists." In his second essay Simpson discusses Faulkner's "myth of the past in the present," his "highly particularized myth of history," and his fable of civilization represented in Yoknapatawpha County.

Faulkner's treatment of two other "myths," race and women, is also considered in this volume. Margaret Walker Alexander writes about Faulkner's attitude toward race and his portrayal of the three races of his native state. "William Faulkner's greatness," she tells us, "may well be his unique achievement in incorporating the American myth about race and the Christian myth of redemption in a body of fiction that is symbolic, humanistic, timeless, and universal." In "Faulkner's Women" Ilse Dusoir Lind brings new understanding to the subject of Faulkner's characterization of women by examining two of his sources, Dr. Louis Berman's *The Glands Regulating Personality* and Dr. Havelock Ellis' *Studies in the Psychology of Sex.* Lind's study of these medical sources reveals that Faulkner was not a literary misogynist but that "he was far more modern than we have allowed, far more audacious than we have perceived, far more reverential of human life as it manifests itself in woman than we have credited."

Faulkner's literary artistry is the subject of two essays by Albert J. Guerard, author of *The Triumph of the Novel.* In "The

Faulknerian Voice" Guerard defines and traces the development of "Faulknerese," prose which shows "a Shakespearean love of language, of playing with language, a Shakespearean love of complication as well as of euphonious music, and of nervous dissonant music too." Guerard also describes the many variants of the Faulknerian voice, the two major ones being Jamesian and Miltonic. "Faulkner was the greatest innovator in the history of American fiction," Guerard writes in his second essay, "because he both freed language from the spare austerity of Hemingway and his imitators, and freed structure from the rectilinear and mimetic controls of the great nineteenth- and twentieth–century realists." Guerard then details several kinds of Faulknerian innovations.

The volume also contains an address made by Associate Vice Chancellor C. E. Noyes welcoming participants to the conference, an event which featured the lectures printed here as well as discussions of such topics as "Faulkner the Artist" and "Faulkner the Man"; tours of Oxford and Lafayette County; films about Faulkner and his environment; slide presentations by J. M. Faulkner, Jo Marshall, and Eva Miller; a Readers' Theatre production, *Voices from Yoknapatawpha*, based on a script arranged by Evans Harrington; and an exhibit of books on William Faulkner submitted by various university presses and hosted by the University Press of Mississippi.

George William Healy, Jr., who attended the University while William Faulkner was postmaster here and was a member of the much-celebrated bridge club which played at the post office, talked about his memories of the novelist as did three members of the Faulkner family—Victoria Fielden Black, J. M. Faulkner, and Dean Faulkner Wells. Several other people who knew Faulkner—Mrs. Mark Hoffman, Aston Holley, William McNeil Reed, William E. Stone, and James W. Webb—also participated on the program. Other activities included a reception at Rowan Oak during which Faulkner's home was dedicated

Introduction

as a National Historic Landmark, a display of books and photographs in the University Library, and exhibitions of watercolors by William C. Baggett, Jr., and multi-media art works by John Davis, William Ralph Dunlap, and William Carey Lester, Jr. The editors hope that all these activities increased the understanding of Faulkner for those who attended the 1977 conference and that the essays printed here will be equally valuable for readers of this volume.

ANN J. ABADIE
University of Mississippi
Oxford, Mississippi

Welcome to Faulkner and Yoknapatawpha, 1977

C. E. NOYES

It is now some fifteen years since William Faulkner walked the streets of Oxford, or stared between the rows of cedars that line the walk to Rowan Oak.

Faulkner's stature as an artist has grown through each of those passing years, not so much because of his posthumous publications (although they are not negligible), but because the understanding of his often difficult work has increased and deepened with the passage of time. I hope it is not self–serving to say that these annual gatherings at the University of Mississippi, now in their fourth summer, have contributed something to that understanding.

Hundreds have come to these conferences from all over America, many from abroad.

Each has come for his own reason. On the lips of some you can almost hear Browning's words from *Memorabilia* (with a slight difference).

Ah, did you once see Faulkner plain?

And did he stop and speak to you?

Some—devotees—have come to touch for themselves a piece of the true cross. Some have come for not much more than a week's outing in very good intellectual company. But we believe our Faulkner Conferences provide something much more than any of these. Something perhaps unique.

Welcome to Faulkner and Yoknapatawpha

Although I played only a very small part in their inception, I had a sudden realization, one evening a few years ago, of what these conferences can mean.

I was attending a meeting of a professional society at the University of Hawaii; and at a cocktail party, I was talking with a quite brilliant young Japanese professor whose field was American literature. When I told him I was from Mississippi, he began at once to talk about teaching Faulkner in his seminar in the American novel. And suddenly a sense of almost lunatic incongruity swept over me. Here I was, sitting on a palm–shaded lanai, drinking mai–tais and nibbling raw fish delicacies, talking to an intense young man who came out of a tradition of samurai and shogun—and who taught the polyglot children of Waikiki Beach about mules, and cotton houses, and red clay hills, and the great brooding wilderness of the Mississippi Delta.

I had rather hesitantly begun, "Ah . . . , if you could show your students a film . . . " when he interrupted me with, "I have *all* of the films; and the best one is called *Faulkner's Mississippi: Land Into Legend.*"

It delighted me of course to know that the work of my respected colleagues and friends here at Ole Miss should be praised so highly. But also it brought home to me what these summer conferences can do for the serious student of Faulkner who comes here with open eyes, and ears, and mind.

Perhaps no other great novelist, almost certainly no other American novelist, is so closely and meaningfully identified with one locale as is William Faulkner with the City of Oxford and the County of Lafayette in Mississippi. The fictional Yoknapatawpha County in which his characters live out their extraordinary lives, although in one sense a universal land, in essence is this North Mississippi hill country which stretches in every direction from the Lafayette County courthouse.

Yet it was Faulkner's genius to take a local habitation and a name, and to give it, not airy nothing, but a reality far more intense than the merely tangible and substantial. His Jefferson is as indestructible as Elsinore. Yoknapatawpha is as eternal as Egdon Heath. Flem Snopes shares Falstaff's immortality, and Eula Varner is gossib to the Wife of Bath.

For those of you who are our guests for the first time, don't expect to find *the* Sutpen house or *the* quicksand bog of *Intruder in the Dust*, or Frenchmen's Bend, or Varner's Store—but what you will see here will make all of these far more real to you as you re–read Faulkner's pages than they have ever been before.

Dr. Joseph Blotner, the Faulkner biographer who spent the spring semester as a visiting professor with us, used to amuse himself by strolling the Oxford streets and identifying "Snopes types" and "Sartoris types" and "Bundren types." He was too wise, however, to seek any *one* original. You would do well to follow his example.

But when you have ridden the dusty back roads of Lafayette County, seen the weather–beaten country stores, walked among the trees of Bailey's Woods, and sweated under a sultry Mississippi sun—when you have in some small measure absorbed the raw material out of which William Faulkner fashioned his marvelous creations—you will have a new and deeper understanding of those creations when you turn to them again.

To say that Faulkner's work is often difficult is a truism. But his is not the double–acrostic, contrived difficulty of James Joyce. Nor is it the mischievous, almost malicious, difficulty of Ezra Pound. The human heart, the human soul, are not simple; and they are not to be simply told.

The—I had almost said "casual" reader of Faulkner, but then perhaps there are no such. Then, the—shall I say "lay reader"?—unaided will find much in Faulkner. But, guided by the perceptions and insights of scholars who have spent years in the study of Faulkner's work, such a reader can find much, much more. Men such as Albert Guerard, Louis Simpson, and Calvin

Brown. Women such as Margaret Walker Alexander and Ilse Dusoir Lind.

And then there are others with something very special indeed to offer: men and women who have known William Faulkner with varying degrees of intimacy—townsmen and townswomen, hunting companions, and relatives. Those who called him "Mr. Faulkner," and those who called him "Bill," and those especially fortunate ones who when children called him "Pappy."

It is one thing to wander, half-lost, through Bailey's Woods. It is another to be taken through them, figuratively hand-in-hand, by guides who know the half-obliterated paths from long memory, or with skilled and trained naturalists to help you see wonders you had missed or had only dimly apprehended.

We want you to feel very welcome here. In what you will experience through the week ahead, we at the University have played only a modest part. It is enough for us to have brought Faulkner students and Faulkner scholars and Faulkner friends together in Faulkner's country. Now we want to be no more than your unobtrusive, but helpful, hosts, as you spend what we hope will be a happy, fulfilling, and rewarding week with William Faulkner in Yoknapatawpha.

The Maker and the Myth:
Faulkner and Yoknapatawpha,
1977

Faulkner's Localism

CALVIN S. BROWN

There is no other place in the world so appropriate for a discussion of Faulkner's localism as the campus of the University of Mississippi. It is a good half mile, at the closest, from Rowan Oak, which is the spot now generally associated with Faulkner; but the campus, not Rowan Oak, is the birthplace of Yoknapatawpha County.

Faulkner's father, Murry, became a business-manager of Ole Miss in 1918, and moved to the campus late in 1919. In spite of Faulkner's trips of longer or shorter duration to Europe, New Orleans, and New York, the house on the campus was his home until he bought Rowan Oak in 1930. During this period he conceived and wrote the first four books of the Yoknapatawpha cycle: *Sartoris, The Sound and the Fury, As I Lay Dying,* and *Sanctuary.* In that house, then, Faulkner's now legendary county was born. I cannot point it out to you because it was torn down many years ago, but if you are staying in the western end of Alumni House, your room may be located on its exact site.

The house where I was born and raised is also gone, though more recently. It was maybe a hundred yards from Faulkner's home, just below the brow of the hill and the end of the new Law Center. I mention this fact as a sort of documentation for my commentary, since much of it is drawn from my own personal knowledge rather than from research or scholarship.

The beginning point for any discussion of Faulkner's localism is so obvious that it cannot be avoided without affectation. In the

3

interview published in the *Paris Review*, Faulkner discussed the early history of his writing with Jean Stein. "Beginning with *Sartoris*," he said, "I discovered that my own little postage stamp of native soil was worth writing about and that I would never live long enough to exhaust it, and by sublimating the actual into the apocryphal I would have complete liberty to use whatever talent I might have to its absolute top." [1] This little postage stamp is, very roughly, the area within about a twenty-mile radius of Oxford, and Faulkner constantly and recognizably uses its roads and streets and square, its railroad, its rural communities, its two rivers and many creeks, its gullied red clay hills, and its springs and cypress swamps, often precisely and literally, but sometimes modified to suit his immediate purposes.

The "postage stamp of native soil" is however a great deal more than a topographical area. It is also flora and fauna, a set of characters and types, a group of dialects and idioms, a set of traditions, a way of life and its accompanying point of view—and even such petty details as a railroad timetable.

Faulkner treats all these things with a minute realistic and even naturalistic accuracy. Lafayette County is the chess board on which he deploys his pieces and plays out his games. And I am inclined to believe that a good deal of the special effect of his work comes from the tension between his literal, earthbound setting and his soaring imagination and flamboyant rhetoric. The setting ballasts the rhetoric and keeps it from flying off into thin air, while the imagination and rhetoric raise the earthy factuality to a mythical level. In Faulkner's work, therefore, there is a constant balance between the genuinely universal and the intensely local. It is to the minuteness and pervasiveness of his localism that my discussion now turns.

---

[1]James B. Meriwether and Michael Millgate (eds.), *Lion in the Garden: Interviews with William Faulkner* (New York: Random House, 1968), 255.

Of all the gross misreadings of Faulkner—and they are many and various—the most incredible to me is Edith Hamilton's contention that he "detests nature." [2] Actually, his love of it is one of the most striking features of his work. Have you ever noticed how much of the action of his novels takes place outdoors, and how little, relatively speaking, is indoors? This proportion not only shows Faulkner's sympathies, it is also a reflection of the traditional way of life of his own local society. Until our recent defection to the plastic, air-conditioned technology which now calls itself civilization, we in the South lived outdoors as much as possible, and from the beginning of the Yoknapatawpha cycle—and even before, in *Soldiers' Pay* and *Mosquitoes*—Faulkner faithfully records this local fact. It is only natural that Old Bayard smokes his cigar on the porch of an evening, and that Miss Jenny is characteristically seen fussing with Isom about the garden. The closest that Young Bayard and Narcissa ever come to a real human companionship and understanding is on a 'possum hunt.

The outdoors in which Faulkner's characters live is no vaguely conceived, gushing notion of "nature," complete with generalized fragrant flowers and feathered songsters. It is, on the contrary, the sharply observed outdoors of northern Mississippi, with its characteristic sights, sounds, and smells—the "miniature suns" of ripening persimmons, a Carolina wren singing in a swamp near a spring flowing from the roots of a beech, the "miration" of the wind in the pines, "the hot still pinewiney silence of the August afternoon." [3] Little vignettes like these could be multiplied almost indefinitely. They are clearly the work of a man who knows and loves the things of which he speaks.

Even the names and terminology are thoroughly localized, for

[2] Edith Hamilton, *The Ever-Present Past* (New York: Norton, 1964), 162.
[3] *Sartoris*, 276; *Sanctuary*, 3–6; *Intruder in the Dust*, 130; *Light in August*, 5. Unless otherwise indicated, all citations of Faulkner's work refer to the hard-cover Random House editions, which are often identical in pagination with paperback editions.

Faulkner's nature is not learned from study and manuals, but from observation and local talk. It is a notorious fact of natural history that local names are highly erratic and confusing. Faulkner's names are always the local ones—whippoorwills for chuck-will's-widows, pin oaks for willow oaks, red birds for cardinals, and even a form of the old country Lord God (a variant of *logcock*) for the pileated woodpecker.—I well remember my first acquaintance with this magnificent bird. I was about four years old when I saw one working on a dying oak in our yard. In great excitement I told our old cook, Aunt Mitty, about it, and she informed me, to my utter bewilderment, that what I had seen was the Lord God. It was only many years later that I got this matter straightened out. Since Faulkner refers to this bird as "the big woodpecker called Lord-to-God by negroes," [4] he may well have had a similar experience.

These locally named plants and animals, like Faulkner's invented characters, inhabit an actual place. This place is, of course, Lafayette County, Mississippi, *alias* Yoknapatawpha County. Some doubts were earlier expressed on this matter, but the evidence is so detailed in its nature and so overwhelming in its quantity that they have been quietly laid to rest. Faulkner is not, of course, literally tied to the geographical facts, and he occasionally alters them to suit his purposes, but, other things being equal, he normally accepts the physical facts of Oxford and of Lafayette County as coinciding with those of his Jefferson and Yoknapatawpha County. I doubt that any theory or even conscious decision entered into this arrangement. Probably he simply imagined his characters playing out their roles in these familiar surroundings. Then, when he described what he had imagined, the local scene necessarily came through.

The main lines are clear enough. Both counties are roughly square, with the county seat approximately in the center. Both

---

[4]*Go Down, Moses*, 202.

have the Tallahatchie River, running roughly from east to west, about twelve miles north of the county seat. Both have a similar river a bit closer to town on the south; in Lafayette County this is now the Yocona (usually pronounced "Yockny"), but Faulkner's county retains and is named for the older form, Yoknapatawpha. Although I never heard this name in my childhood, I have a cheap atlas, published in 1932 but obviously slapped together from older maps, which so labels it. Both counties have main roads running to the west, northwest, north, northeast, east, and southeast, but not to the southwest—at least, not in Faulkner's time.

Faulkner's two maps of his domain, in *Absalom, Absalom!* and the Viking *Portable Faulkner*, show the similarities very clearly. In fact, they differ from the actual maps of the early part of the century in only two significant ways. First of all, Faulkner's maps are much more schematic than the actual ones, with the roads and rivers straighter, the road running parallel to the railroad all the way out of the county instead of crossing it a bit south of the Tallahatchie, as it actually does, and other little simplifications of the same sort. I take this as simply another manifestation of the general principle that the artist always desires and creates neater patterns than the rather messy ones created by life itself. (At the University of Virginia, Faulkner commented that "any writer worth his salt is convinced that he can create much better people than God can.")[5] The other real change is that, if we accept Faulkner's accurate figures, we know that Joanna Burden's house (in the community of St. Paul's) was two miles from the courthouse clock, and the flag-stop of Sartoris Station was four miles from town. But this does not really work out on either of Faulkner's own maps, where the station is considerably more than twice as far from the

---

[5]Frederick L. Gwynn and Joseph L. Blotner (eds.), *Faulkner in the University: Class Conferences at the University of Virginia, 1957–1958* (New York: Random House, 1965), 118.

square as the Burden house. There is no reason to expect
Faulkner to be pedantic in his sketch of a map, of course, though
he was a good draftsman and—what is even more important in
this connection—a good sign painter. It is possible that he drew
square maps and the publishers compressed them laterally to
make the rectangles which they needed. At any rate, they would
be truer to Faulkner's distances (and the actual distances of St.
Paul's and College Hill Station) if they were laterally expanded
to make them squares. But I imagine that he would find this
whole question either tedious or amusing, depending on his
mood at the moment.

Other changes in the actual landscape are clearly made for
very real and obvious reasons. In *Light in August*, Joe Christmas
walks from town to his cabin, and his trip and route are minutely
described.[6] Faulkner gives no street names, but the route is
unmistakable for any old-timer in Oxford, and can be clearly
followed today. Joe left the barbershop at the northwestern
corner of the square, went down Jackson Avenue, turned left a
very short block up South Sixth Street to Van Buren Avenue,
and then turned right on Van Buren and followed it to the
railroad station. All this is precisely described, with accurate
details on the ups and downs and even the steepness of the
grades. At the station Joe crossed the railroad tracks and went
into a path leading through a mile of woods. Actually, at the time
of *Light in August* and, with slight differences, even today, he
would have gone up a sidewalk, first through woods and then
past faculty houses. When he paused and looked towards town,
he was at the upper corner of my old front yard, and he would
have gone on through the campus from there. It is plain,
though, that Faulkner does not want a state university in his
typical small town, and so he simply expurgates it, letting Joe
re-enter the actual landscape when he leaves the campus, about
where the University Hospital now stands.

---

[6]*Light in August*, 105–110.

But Faulkner did not dispense with the campus of Ole Miss entirely. He merely moved it from his Jefferson to his Oxford, which is a town some fifty miles from Jefferson, with a location which is geometrically impossible, and is, in his fiction, the seat of the university. When Horace Benbow went to the Ole Miss campus in *Sanctuary* to check up on Temple Drake, he got off the train at the station and followed the route that Joe Christmas would actually have followed, up the hill on the sidewalk and on to the main grove with three paths running across it, one of them leading to the post office, exactly as the campus was in the late 1920s.[7] It would be hard to find a clearer example in fiction anywhere of a minute use of the actual scenes familiar to the author, combined with complete freedom in modifying to suit his purposes.

Many other journeys are given with similar detail and accuracy—that of Mink Snopes from the square to the station on Jackson Avenue, and that of Horace Benbow from the station to the square, on Van Buren Avenue; Mink Snopes's trip from Holly Springs (called Memphis Junction) to Jefferson by a devious route of road, creek bottom, and railroad; the route of Joe Christmas's attempted escape from the square to Hightower's house; Dilsey's walk to church; and the Bundren family's first view of Jefferson from the ridge to the southeast, followed by their trip on into town.[8] It should be noted that only when they come in sight of their goal do they enter any recognizable topography. Otherwise, the geography of *As I Lay Dying* is an anomaly at odds with that of both Faulkner's Yoknapatawpha County and the actual Lafayette County. This fact seems striking enough to be worth mentioning, but I can offer no explanation for it.

Faulkner also uses a considerable number of clearly recog-

<hr>

[7]*Sanctuary*, 166–67.
[8]*The Mansion*, 34–35; *Sartoris*, 165–66; *The Mansion*, 396–407; *Light in August*, 435*ff.*; *The Sound and the Fury*, 362–64; *As I Lay Dying*, 216–21.

nizable places, many of them now totally gone or modified beyond recognition—places like the old Oxford power plant just south of the station, the planing mill on the railroad south of town, the old brick jail, the railroad trestle over Hurricane Creek, the cemetery (which he shifts around a bit for obvious reasons), Buffaloe's Café, Chilton's Drug Store, a striking view from near College Hill, and the big ditch behind the old Oxford schoolhouse.[9]

Some proper names are simply adopted and used. Among these are the village of Taylor eight miles south of Oxford, Hurricane Creek (some five miles to the north), Freedman Town, Holly Springs (when it is not called Memphis Junction), Memphis itself, and the Tallahatchie River. Some other names are only slightly disguised. Yellowleaf Creek is changed to Whiteleaf; Chilton's Drug Store becomes Christian's, and College Hill is perfunctorily disguised as Seminary Hill. Other names are totally changed. Water Valley is called both Mottson and Mottstown; Buffaloe's Café is changed to Deacon's, and Grand Junction, Tennessee, is rechristened Parsham. Finally, there are some places which Faulkner did not name, but we can. The branch that runs through the Compson place and plays such an important part in *The Sound and the Fury* is Burney's Branch; the joint near the station where, in *Sanctuary*, Gowan Stevens first gets drunk, was named The Shack; the community at the edge of which Joanna Burden lives is St. Paul's.[10] These

---

[9]Flem Snopes stole the brass fittings from this power plant (*The Town*, 9*ff.*). Byron Bunch worked at the planing mill (*Light in August*, 27 and passim). The old jail appears in many works, most conspicuously in *Sanctuary* and *Intruder in the Dust*. The trestle is in *The Mansion*, 404. The cemetery appears in *Sartoris*, 372 and a number of other places. Buffaloe's Café is Deacon's place (*Sartoris*, 122*ff.*), and Chilton's Drug Store appears (as Christian's) in *The Town*, 154–59 and the short story "Uncle Willy." The view is described in *The Town*, 315–17. The big ditch is involved in Percy Grimm's pursuit of Joe Christmas (*Light in August*, 435) and is also the place where the deadly half-breed children of Byron Snopes cooked and ate an expensive lapdog (*The Town*, 362–64).

[10]Since many of these names occur repeatedly, it seems needless to document them here. They are all documented in my *A Glossary of Faulkner's South* (New Haven: Yale, 1976).

examples by no means exhaust the possibilities, but I believe that they are sufficient to show how intensely Faulkner's imagination lived in the local scene and how consistently he drew his literary sustenance from it.

A great deal of the feeling of down-to-earth reality and immediacy which Faulkner's fiction produces is probably due to his long familiarity and emotional involvement with the places where it all happens. We get this feeling strongly in works like *Sartoris, The Sound and the Fury,* and *Light in August*—and we miss it conspicuously in *A Fable.* Part of the difference is doubtless due to the fact that *A Fable* was an abstract concept in the first place; note that it is not only an allegory, but is also the only novel that the mature Faulkner wrote from a detailed outline. Another part is doubtless due to the fact that he knew the South in general from thirty years of living there, whereas he knew France only from about three months as a tourist. A country which one visits in this way never seems quite real.

When Balzac was writing *Eugénie Grandet,* a friend came to discuss a problem with him. Balzac stood it as long as he could, and then broke in, saying, "But let's get back to real life. Consider Eugénie Grandet." Many of Faulkner's remarks show that his best creations had exactly that sort of reality for him. They became as real as their settings.

The unforgettable and ultimately nostalgic experiences of childhood form particularly strong associations with the places where they occurred. In spite of all the changes of five or six decades, for example, I cannot walk up the hill from the station to Alumni House without a feeling that I can experience nowhere else on earth. This is the sort of feeling that Faulkner had for his settings. He was perhaps fortunate in having two childhoods—one real and one vicarious. In his home in town he and his two brothers of nearly the same age, along with a whole group of boys in the neighborhood, had a rich, busy, and imaginative boyhood. This was, luckily, before the age of highly

11

organized "play" concentrating on supervised team sports played with a professional approach. The memoirs of Faulkner's brothers John and Murry provide a fine picture of these boys finding and inventing their own pastimes.[11] At one point they built an airplane and Billy, acting as pilot, got into it and had the other boys throw it from a high bank. The craft achieved limited success—a short vertical flight to the bottom of a ditch. Another time the boys painted a playhouse and, inevitably, each other. They found an old Civil War cap-and-ball revolver, stole powder from their father's shotgun shells, loaded it to the gills, and fired it off, sensationally and consternationally. They hunted and fished and, in general, lived fine imaginative and unregimented lives.

The vicarious childhood came when the Falkners moved here to the campus. Here a group of four neighborhood boys, including Faulkner's brother Dean, took shape. The oldest of our bunch was ten years younger than Faulkner; I, the youngest, was twelve years younger. We had a childhood and early youth very much like that of the older Falkner brothers, and though William Faulkner was not, of course, a regular, full-time member of our group, he did participate in a good many of our activities, especially our Sunday afternoon cross-country paper-chases. I have recorded these things elsewhere[12] and cannot go into them now except to point out that this vicarious re-experiencing of childhood as a young adult doubtless reinforced his emotional attachments to the local scene and contributed to his ability to portray with profound sympathy, but at the same time with the necessary aesthetic distance, the experiences of Bayard and Ringo, of Chick Mallison and Alec Sander, and, in his final apotheosis of childhood, of Lucius Priest.

---

[11]John Faulkner, *My Brother Bill: An Affectionate Reminiscence* (New York: Trident, 1963); Murry C. Falkner, *The Falkners of Mississippi: A Memoir* (Baton Rouge: LSU Press, 1967).
[12]James W. Webb and A. Wigfall Green (eds.), *William Faulkner of Oxford* (Baton Rouge: LSU Press, 1965), 40–48.

How far Faulkner's people derive from the local scene is a question that has been much discussed. Some things are quite obvious to anyone who knows both the Oxford of the 1920s and 1930s and Faulkner's fiction. There can be no question that Gavin Stevens owes a good deal to Phil Stone, but that he also owes a great deal to the fictional imagination. And he is the only one of the major characters for whom even a significant partial prototype exists. (Popeye, in *Sanctuary,* diverges so far from the actual Memphis gangster that the latter is, at most, a hint rather than a model.) A few minor characters are taken over without much change. Deacon (of Deacon's Café, in *Sartoris*) and Uncle Willy (in the short story of that name and in various references to Christian's Drug Store scattered through other works) are obvious examples. In a broad way, however, we can cover the use of local characters with a few very loose generalizations. Faulkner invented his principal characters, and even for his minor ones he seldom drew portraits, though he did, very occasionally, take hints.

The hints of this general type that he took most often, however, were not of characters, but of incidents. Over and over again the old-timer from Oxford will find things in the fiction expanded and reworked from events that actually took place. The business of leading mules onto the railroad in order to have them hit by freight trains and thus to collect damages from the railroad—which plays a considerable role in "Mule in the Yard" and the parallel episode in *The Town*—actually happened in Oxford and came out in a lawsuit. There are many such "sources" for elements of Faulkner's plots. Many of them are not recorded anywhere, but some elderly person who really knows Oxford gossip over the last sixty years (as I do not) could write a very entertaining, though possibly libelous, book setting them all forth.

One matter in which Faulkner very definitely does *not* use the local scene is that of houses. Even without his maps, we could easily tell the approximate location of the Benbow, Compson, and Sartoris houses, for example, but we cannot point to any actual buildings that inspired them. The identifications that we now hear have their basis in tourist-promotion, not responsible scholarship. I suppose it is probably much easier to put invented people into invented houses than it is mentally to evict one's neighbors and move strangers into their houses. At any rate, Faulkner never tried to do this. The only house of any of his important characters that I think I know is that of Joanna Burden, out past St. Paul's, and it burned down (as did hers) long ago. I never knew whose house it was, and I doubt if Faulkner did either.

One might talk forever about Faulkner's local scenes and his attachment to them, and, since they are also the local scenes of my own childhood, I am sorely tempted to do so. But there are other things to be considered, and we must move on.

One of these other considerations is Faulkner's extensive and accurate use of local dialects and idioms. This subject, however, requires a preliminary clearing of the air. It is on the basis of this aspect of Faulkner that many critics have pigeon-holed him as a local colorist. Actually, he is nothing of the sort, and the reason can be simply stated.

Let us compare Faulkner with another southern writer, Augustus Baldwin Longstreet. It seems appropriate to compare Longstreet and Faulkner, especially since they are buried in the Oxford cemetery only a few hundred yards apart. Longstreet is almost a classic case of a local colorist, as noted in the following sentence quoted from "The Fight," a sketch in his *Georgia Scenes:* "In the younger days of the Republic there lived in the county of ——— two men, who were admitted on all hands to be the very *best men* in the county; which, in the Georgia vocabulary, means they could flog any other two men in the county." Observe that Longstreet italicizes the words *best men* and then explains to his readers what they mean "in the Georgia vocabulary." This approach makes it clear that he and his readers are sophisticated men of the world looking down with tolerant amusement at the antics of a bunch of local yokels. This is the typical stance of the local colorist. No matter how affectionately indulgent he may be towards his characters, the collusion against them, the complacent wink from author to reader, is always there. And the creatures who are so observed are not really people—they are not human, but only quaint.

Faulkner's attitude is totally different. He lives in and with his characters and makes no attempt to cancel his little postage stamp—a fact that presents difficulties to many readers. He never explains what a *fur piece* or a *loggerhead* or a *shikepoke* means "in the Mississippi vocabulary." He is no more concerned with explaining the small-town southern use of *Miss* with a married woman's first name for the benefit of New Yorkers than a New York writer is concerned with explaining *subway* for the benefit of Hottentots. Since his characters are real, he can let them speak for themselves, as they really speak, without auctorial winks or exegesis. If the reader does not understand the language of Old Man Falls or Lucas Beauchamp or Lena Grove, that is the reader's problem, not Faulkner's. If he has never geared up a plow mule or lined out a hymn or run a trotline, he is too culturally deprived to understand parts of Faulkner, and Faulkner offers him no help. That is why I decided to make a glossary of such things while they are still known. The job was necessary because it seems certain that Faulkner's fiction will outlive the world in which it is set. In some aspects, like mule agriculture, it has already done so.

Few things show Faulkner's localism as clearly as his accurate use of local speech—accurate in vocabulary, syntax, and (as far as normal printing will permit) in pronunciation. This accuracy is no accident, as two of his remarks at the University of Virginia will show. When a student there asked him how many different dialects he distinguished in his work, he answered: "I would say there are three. The dialect, the diction of the educated semi-metropolitan white southerner, the dialect of the hill backward southerner, and the dialect of the Negro—four, the dialect of the Negro who has been influenced by the northern cities, who has been to Chicago and Detroit." [13] In reply to another question, he said, "You've got to see . . . the scenes you describe." This is a matter that I have already discussed at some length, but he continued: "You've got to hear the voice speaking the speech that you put down. You have to hear the vernacular he speaks in, rather than to think of the speech and then translate it into the vernacular." [14]

Any attempt to discuss the language of Faulkner's characters in detail will necessarily become a technical linguistic treatise with an added dash of sociology—a mixture which would be quite unpalatable on an occasion like this. All that can or should be done here is to indicate the main lines that such a discussion might take, with particular attention to localism.

The novel with the clearest, most exact, and most literarily effective differentiations in the speech of its characters is *Sanctuary*. (In general, I avoid such dogmatic statements, but this is one that I am willing to defend.) A brief consideration of some of the characters of this novel will show that Faulkner actually differentiated a great many more than the four dialects and idioms that he specified in his offhand answer at Virginia.

First of all, we note that not all the speech is local or regional. Lee Goodwin has knocked around the world in the armed services, done a hitch in Leavenworth, and generally has few local connections, though he has been moonshining at the Old Frenchman Place for four years. He speaks a sort of cosmopolitan substandard English, laced with occasional underworld terms. Ruby, his common-law wife, has been around a good deal

[13]Gwynn and Blotner (eds.), *Faulkner in the University*, 125.
[14]*Ibid.*, 181.

too, keeping up with him. But her background is rural southern. Her dialect has been toned down considerably, however, and in general she speaks English much like Lee's except that in addition to his underworld terms she uses occasional fine Elizabethan phrases, as when she calls Temple Drake a "little doll-faced slut." [15]

Horace Benbow is incurably literary, in the ironic sense of the term. He is given to arty pseudo-poetic flights like "reaffirmation of the old ferment" and "the slain flowers, the delicate dead flowers and tears." [16] Brought up in Jefferson, he was educated at Oxford University, and his speech is a reflection of his character more than of his actual background.

Temple Drake, the daughter—as she never tires of reminding everyone—of a Jackson judge, speaks basically an upperclass southern idiom, individualized by the college slang and flapper cuteness of the late twenties in such expressions as "You mean old thing" and "Be a sport." [17]

Popeye and Tommy form an interesting pair. Both are mentally below par and both talk primarily in set phrases, but this is as far as the similarity goes. Popeye has a southern background, but the element of his speech that expresses his character is laconic and menacing, and the element drawn from his associations is the smarty-contemptuous jargon of gangsters. Tommy, on the other hand, is pure rural Yoknapatawpha County, with such set phrases as "I be dawg ef . . . " (he uses this three times on a single page)[18] and "Durn my hide." His pronunciations include *skeered* (for *scared*), *spile* (for *spoil*), *hit* (for *it*), *tromp* (for *tramp*, meaning "step"), *helt* (for *held*), *hisn* (for *his*), and a host of other regionalisms and localisms. Incidentally, Bobby, the waitress-prostitute of *Light in August*,

---

[15]*Sanctuary*, 68.
[16]*Ibid.*, 13, 14.
[17]*Ibid.*, 65, 57.
[18]*Ibid.*, 44.

with her arrested development and mechanically iterated phrases, is very much like Tommy except that her idiom is that of the Memphis petty underworld.

Perhaps the finest linguistic *tour de force* in *Sanctuary* is the conversation at the three madams' drinking party after Red's funeral. The ladies speak a fundamentally southern dialect, modified by contributions from the national brothel culture. Miss Reba and her two friends start out in a prim and affected imitation of what they take to be elegant, high-society conversation, but as they warm up to their subjects, begin to talk shop, and progress from beer to gin, the veneer begins to crack and peel and the idiom of the whorehouse emerges more and more clearly, often contrasting amusingly with the affectation of respectability. Faulkner's presentation of the gradual progression from the madams' affected speech to their real idiom is a masterpiece involving the speech of both the region and the milieu.

I shall have to pass over many other aspects of the linguistic differentiation of the characters in *Sanctuary*, but not without at least mentioning the fine combination of pomposity, rural dialect, and general illiteracy which characterizes the speech of state senator Clarence Snopes.

As we have seen, the types of speech that Faulkner uses go very far beyond the four that he mentioned. Furthermore, they never serve the purpose of mere quaintness, as they would for a local colorist. They are essentially devices of characterization, though they sometimes serve for humor or to keep the different backgrounds, social class, or attitudes of two contrasting characters visible throughout a conversation—or, more usually, a confrontation—without having to harp on the subject.

In other novels we find the same thing, though there are only two characters that really call for further comment. These are Gavin Stevens and his friend Ratliff. These men have two traits in common: both are loquacious, and both are aware of their own language in a way that most characters—and people—are not.

They are, however, clearly differentiated, though neither ever strays far from their common base of Yoknapatawpha.

Gavin is an excellent Greek scholar, educated at Harvard and Heidelberg, but he has never renounced his local linguistic heritage. His general speech is highly educated American, with (as with everyone) regional overtones. He is also in politics in a minor way, and Faulkner comments on his ability deliberately to speak pure rural Yoknapatawphan when it suits his purposes. This linguistic dualism is an old political device. Some fifty years ago, I heard Governor Bilbo deliver two speeches within a few hours of each other, one here on the Ole Miss campus, the other at a Lafayette County dinner-on-the-grounds political rally. He spoke two quite different languages on these two occasions. He was neither as educated nor as cultivated as Gavin Stevens, and hence on the campus he could not quite match Stevens's most standard literary usage, but he did a very good job of trying to, and ended up with something between Gavin's sophisticated and Ratliff's normal usage. Out in the county, he changed to something about halfway between Ratliff and the rural ineptness of Tommy. Whatever one might think of Bilbo otherwise, one had to admire his command of linguistic tone and associations.

Ratliff speaks the pure idiom of the rural countryman of this region, if we discount (as we must) his distressing efforts to improve his language in *The Mansion*. Linguistically, he belongs with Tull and Bookwright and other such rural yeomen, who are not, of course, "poor whites." What differentiates him from such men is not linguistic but personal. He has a shrewdness, a humor, which shows in only occasional flashes in their speech, but is a constant element in his. And, more particularly, he is constantly aware of his language, deliberately manipulating it for ironic or comic effect, as aware of the *mot juste* as Flaubert. But he does not go outside his native stock; he simply uses the basic local language of Tull and Bookwright far more skillfully and poetically, in the large sense of the word, than they can. The proof of this fact lies in the many scenes where we see that they can appreciate and understand what Ratliff does with language, though it lies far beyond anything that they could ever do. He is a cabinetmaker who can take a bungling carpenter's tools and do a beautiful job with them.

The discussion of Faulkner's dialects and idioms has already involved some comment on his rich variety of characters and types. There is no need to try to list or analyze them in detail, but a few general points need to be made. First of all, Faulkner has an extraordinarily wide range of types and social classes—as wide as Chaucer's in the *Canterbury Tales*. But as wide as the range is, the types are indigenous to his own little postage stamp of native soil. Although this society is far more pluralistic than many critics, with their silly stereotypes for the South, are able or willing to realize, there are nevertheless outsiders who are not and cannot be assimilated. Whether they be, like Camus' *étranger*, of indigenous origin, or whether they be outsiders geographically, they stick out like the proverbial sore thumb. Faulkner's Mississippi is not, and never was, of course, the closed society that James Silver pretended, but it does have its limits along with its variations. These limits, however, are not mere prejudices—or, if they are, so are the limits of all other societies.

Fundamentally, outsiders may be either indigenous or exotic, since they are simply persons who cannot accept or be accepted by the society in which they live. In a very crude way, this amounts to saying that they do not even approximately fit any of the generally recognized local types. A good specimen of the simple outsider from outside is Matt Levitt, the drifting Ohio auto mechanic and Golden Gloves champion to whom Gavin Stevens loses one of his invariably disastrous fist-fights. After a brief sojourn of fighting and hell raising, Levitt is fired by the garage where he works and, by a mutually acceptable agreement with the sheriff, leaves town—with obscene vituperation, of course.[19] He was simply a total alien to Jefferson, and it to him. Today, unfortunately, he would doubtless fit in at almost any small-town drag strip in the South.

Joanna Burden presents a very different case. She is the third generation from her carpetbagger grandfather and is an outsider by choice and profession. She is so full of mental ambivalencies that she would probably be an outsider anywhere, but her stubbornly retained attitudes of the New England of eighty years earlier make her totally unassimilable in Jefferson. In fact, she lives in a largely self-created past as much as does a southern outsider, Hightower, also in *Light in August*. Neither has any chance except a change from within. Life finally breaks in on the cocoon which Hightower has spun for himself, but it is death that breaks in on Joanna.

The native outsiders are more interesting than the foreign ones, though Cleanth Brooks has discussed them so thoroughly in his various comments on the sense of community in Faulkner that not much more needs to be said. Hence I shall mention only two more cases.

Quentin Compson's alienation is entirely internal, dating from puberty, and entirely unlocal. Fundamentally, he has rejected puberty itself and maintained a quarrel against the sexual nature of mankind. He would be an alien in any community.

Linda Snopes has acquired her alienation. Conceived by a dirt road near Frenchman's Bend and raised in Jefferson, having her mind "formed" by Gavin Stevens, she has gone to Greenwich Village, married a Jewish sculptor, become a Communist, fought in the Spanish Civil War, and returned to Jefferson, where she tries to foment communism. She does not meet much opposition or sense of outrage, but a far more frustrating apathy and incomprehension, and Faulkner treats her efforts with

---

[19]*The Town*, 197.

indulgent amusement. Finally, after secretly arranging for her putative father's murder (a thoroughly commendable act, by the way), she departs from Jefferson, presumably forever, in a new Jaguar. Ironically, Russian critics, utterly missing Faulkner's wry amusement, latch onto her communism and make her a heroic figure. Like many other tendentious critics, they also misrepresent some of the actual events of the plot in order to make their ideas work.[20]

The main point to be noted about Faulkner's treatment of types and characters, then, is that those of his own town and county are taken to be a norm, and those who do not conform to this norm, whether condemned or praised, are seen as aberrations. It should be added that the norms of ideas and conduct are capable of development and improvement. Bayard Sartoris, in "An Odor of Verbena," and Chick Mallison, in *Intruder in the Dust*, are initiated into manhood by commendably breaking with their traditions.

These regional and local traditions are, in general, assumed in Faulkner's works, and this fact is another aspect of his localism. It is also significant that those who can break or admirably expand the tradition are those brought up in it, not outside reformers. But it is misleading to speak of the tradition, since Faulkner's society is far more pluralistic than many readers and critics have realized. It must be emphasized that it is not a matter of different social or economic classes having different traditions and ideals. Bank president Sartoris and pauper Old

---

[20]YA. N. Zasurskij, *Amerikanskaya literatura XX veka: Nekotorye aspekti literaturnogo protsessa* (Moscow: Moscow University, 1966), 402–404. Though Linda Snopes goes to work in a shipyard in Pascagoula "right after New Year's, 1941" (*The Mansion*, 246) and Hitler did not invade Russia until June 2, 1941, Zasurskij says, "but when Hitler attacked the Soviet Union, she entered a shipbuilding yard . . ." (p. 402, my translation). Strangely enough, the Russian translation of *The Mansion* (*Osobnyak*, p. 247) has Linda going to work in Pascagoula "shortly after New Year's, 1942" (my translation). The element of Linda's communism is similarly treated heroically by B. I. Kolesnikov in *Kurs lektsij po istorii zarubezhnoj literatury XX veka* (Moscow: Vyschaya SHkola, 1965), 676–78.

Man Falls share the same tradition, as does the poor white Wash Jones. In fact, Wash finally kills Sutpen for betraying their common tradition of *noblesse oblige*. Ratliff and Gavin Stevens have inherited some of this same tradition, but much modified and often viewed with skepticism. Even the Snopes clan, often thought of as having no tradition, have a very strong one, but it is uniquely that of their type. Ratliff comments that just as you have the expert admired by connoisseurs in any field, the lawyers' lawyer or the actors' actor, it is the ambition of every Snopes to become THE son of a bitch's son of a bitch.[21] This is eminently true, and has been since the time of the founder of the clan, Ab Snopes of Civil War days, in *The Unvanquished*. Though no one puts it quite that way, the Snopes clan represents the irruption of a new, more universal tradition into the ancient ones of Yoknapatawpha County.

It seems appropriate to close these remarks by rounding out the circle and returning from abstractions like traditions to literal localisms like places and names. The train schedules will serve this purpose nicely. I had always realized vaguely that the trains through Jefferson ran on the same schedules as those through Oxford during my boyhood. For a while there were three passenger trains a day in each direction, but the basic timetable from about 1915 till passenger service was discontinued in 1941 called for two each way every day. There were occasional slight changes, but the general pattern remained constant: a train south at about 10:30 A.M., one north at about 3:00 P.M., one south around 9:00 P.M., and one north about 3:00 A.M. This is the schedule on which Faulkner's fictional trains operate, and often, though not always, the trains are called accurately by their official numbers. Often, also, there is no fictional or literary reason for the schedules. To take a single example, in *Light in*

---

[21]*The Mansion*, 87.

August,[22] when Doc Hines and his wife decide to go from Mottstown (Water Valley) to Jefferson, some twenty miles to the north, it is already about four in the afternoon; so they have just missed the northbound train. They eat supper, go to the station, see the southbound train come through about nine o'clock, and wait in the station until they catch the northbound train for Jefferson about two or three in the morning. No fictional purpose is served by this wait and this schedule—except the all-important one of making Faulkner's fiction real and actual in his own mind.

And this, fundamentally, rather than any pedantry or mere local color, is the purpose, the reason for the existence, of all Faulkner's localism. He imagined his plots as taking place on his own little postage stamp of native soil, and he recorded accurately what he had imagined.

---

[22]*Light in August*, 339–41.

The Faulknerian Voice

ALBERT J. GUERARD

It's with no little humility that I venture to speak in Oxford about the Faulknerian voice. I was comparably embarrassed, several years ago, to speak to a British audience in Canterbury, in my thick American accent, about the voices of Dickens and Conrad. I could take some consolation in the fact that Conrad's accent was even less British than mine, but this was hardly true for Dickens. My plight may seem as serious in talking about the "voice" of such a very southern writer. My excuse or justification is that I mean by *voice* the interior voice we hear in good written prose, which may be very different from the speaking voice heard by family and friends. Conrad was totally incapable of rendering, in actual speech or in the one public reading of his life, the beautiful running rhythms of his written prose. And I suspect this was true, though less so, of Faulkner—though I talked with him only once, for perhaps an hour, in 1946. Even the best of the recordings (while they at times convey the true breathless rush of sound) do not do justice to the voice we hear in Faulkner's best liberated prose.

I will begin by reiterating the truism that every great writer has a recognizable personal voice, and any lover of Faulkner would recognize as his almost any page written after 1929, and many pages written before that. This voice may have various tonalities. The Joycean word-play of *Pylon* is rather different from the rhetoric, almost Shakespearean, of the virtually contemporary *Absalom, Absalom!* Yet there is an underlying or overriding Faulknerian voice in both novels. A writer's personal voice is an intimate reflection or expression of his mind and temperament, of his deepest core of being, externalized in the "shape and ring of sentences" (Conrad), in the way his mind moves, a reflection too of his anxieties and obsessions. I like to make a distinction between *voice* and *style*, and to suggest that what we have (as we compare *Pylon* and *Absalom, Absalom!*) are different *styles*. I will try to illustrate the distinction with a few words from my lecture on the Conradian voice:

> How then can we distinguish *voice* from *style*? I define style as language and the conventions of language which are not determined by an author's own temperament and personal exigencies; a certain style may be shared by a number of writers, though each will have his individual voice. A number of eighteenth century poets imitate rather closely Milton's blank verse, as does the Wordsworth of *The Excursion.* Many of the rhetorical devices are the same, yet Wordsworth's long paragraphs have their own particular gait. And his double negatives (which usually have the effect of seeming doubly negative) often betray a deep-lying insecurity that is altogether his own. Thus we hear Wordsworth's own voice even when he adopts rather closely a Miltonic style. Style is, more than voice, acquired and conventional.[1]

Voice then is the expression of temperament, and of an inward self that may be radically different from the persona known to family and friends. This inward self, in Faulkner, was notably aloof, evasive, ironic, involuted, infinitely complex, unmistakably self-protective and private, yet playful too, protecting itself by means of abstraction and complicated syntax and elaborate narrative structure. Faulkner at his best, like Conrad at his best, maintained considerable distance between himself and his fic-

---

[1]"The Conradian Voice," in Norman Sherry (ed.), *Joseph Conrad: A Commemoration,* (London, 1976), 4.

tional world, and between himself and his reader; a psychoanalyst would perhaps speak of defense mechanisms. Perhaps the fullest effort to define Faulkner's style—or, as I would put it, voice—is that of Walter Slatoff in *A Quest for Failure*. Slatoff notes tension and conflict at every level, paradox and oxymoron, blocked feeling, an unwillingness to close in on things. What he fails to see is that tension is often relieved through prose rhythm—the notorious running rhythms that can now and then have the effect of a broken record.

No one should forget Conrad Aiken's admirable early effort to define Faulkner's style, which he compares to the "exuberant and tropical luxuriance of sound which Jim Europe's jazz band used to exhale, like a jungle of rank creepers and ferocious blooms taking shape before one's eyes—magnificently and endlessly intervolved, glisteningly and ophidianly in motion, coil sliding over coil, and leaf and flower forever magically interchanging." [2] Some critics have spoken, too simplistically, of Faulkner's relationship to the traditions of southern oratory, and there are indeed moments in *Intruder in the Dust* and *A Fable* when the writer appears to be perched on a stump. Faulkner himself ascribed his peculiarities to an effort to encompass everything, get all experience onto the page; but this also seems rather too simple. Surely we have, beyond question, a Shakespearean love of language, of playing with language, a Shakespearean love of complication as well as of euphonious music, and of nervous dissonant music too.

Most writers must discover, by long trial and error, their own personal voices. They must discover the particular combination of novelistic material and novelistic technique that will be truly congenial, that will energize their imaginations and release those true voices. Thus Conrad tried in vain, in the 1890s, to

---

[2]"William Faulkner: The Novel as Form," first printed in *The Atlantic Monthly* (November, 1939), reprinted in Linda W. Wagner (ed.), *William Faulkner: Four Decades of Criticism* (Michigan State University), 134.

write of sexual maladjustment and artistic frustration in an urban setting, and to write objectively in the third person.[3] He needed instead to discover his own true fictional world of isolated men tested and threatened by deterioration in jungles or on the high seas, and also had to discover a point of view that would allow him to treat his material at once intimately and with detachment. He had to discover, that is, Marlow's or other interposed screening consciousness. And so Faulkner, who was not born to write of weary and witty sophisticates such as Januarius Jones, or even of New Orleans Bohemians, had to work his way past the New Orleans sketches and *Soldiers' Pay* and *Mosquitoes*, past both Sherwood Anderson and Swinburne.

Faulkner has obviously discovered his own world in *Sartoris* (and *Flags in the Dust*), with V. K. Suratt and Byron and Flem Snopes, with Oxford / Jefferson, the McCallum clan, and the long hours of drinking on the topsy-turvy farm, where alcohol overcomes the barriers of neurosis, race, class. But the discovery is also of distance and point of view. Here too, Conrad's example is illuminating. For a brief moment, in 1896, in the manuscript of "The Rescuer," Conrad breaks free of narrative inhibitions. An "I" addresses distant figures, deep in the historic past: "Did you follow with your ghostly eyes the quest of this obscure adventurer of yesterday you shades of forgotten adventurers who in leather jerkins and sweating under steel helmets attacked with long rapiers the palisades of the strange heathen, or musket on shoulder and match in cock guarded lonely forts built upon the banks of rivers that command good trade." [4]

Just so in *Sartoris* Faulkner recognizes that he as a writer is free to do anything. Why should he not be a "Homer of the cotton fields," a Homer who could put into his poem a long catalogue or anything else he pleased? And now we find, in the

---

[3]See Albert J. Guerard, *Conrad the Novelist* (Cambridge, Mass., 1958), 92–98.
[4]The published version adds five commas to the sentence, and so destroys its running rhythm: *The Rescue* (Kent ed.), 94.

famous apostrophe to the mule, the true Faulknerian voice speaking in full-throated ease. We find the running rhythms and the delight in absurd analogy, the extravagance that can even evoke, for this apocalyptic mule, St. Anthony in the desert. I will quote only part of this familiar flight. The first sentence is clear, classical, controlled, precise writing. It is with the third sentence that we see fully anticipated the Faulkner of the 1930s and beyond:

Round and round the mule went, setting its narrow, deer-like feet delicately down in the hissing cane-pith, its neck bobbing limber as a section of rubber hose in the collar, with its trace-galled flanks and flopping, lifeless ears and its half-closed eyes drowsing venomously behind pale lids, apparently asleep with the monotony of its own motion. Some Homer of the cotton fields should sing the saga of the mule and of his place in the South. He it was, more than any other one creature or thing, who, steadfast to the land when all else faltered before the hopeless juggernaut of circumstance, impervious to conditions that broke men's hearts because of his venomous and patient preoccupation with the immediate present, won the prone South from beneath the iron heel of Reconstruction and taught it pride again through humility, and courage through adversity overcome; who accomplished the well-nigh impossible despite hopeless odds, by sheer and vindictive patience. Father and mother he does not resemble, sons and daughters he will never have; vindictive and patient (it is a known fact that he will labor ten years willingly and patiently for you, for the privilege of kicking you once); solitary but without pride, self-sufficient but without vanity; his voice is his own derision. Outcast and pariah, he has neither friend, wife, mistress, nor sweetheart; celibate, he is unscarred, possesses neither pillar nor desert cave, he is not assaulted by temptations nor flagellated by dreams nor assuaged by vision; faith, hope and charity are not his.[5]

And so on for another page. This may not be the best "Faulk-

---

[5] In *Flags in the Dust* the second sentence read (p. 313): "Some Cincinnatus of the cotton fields should contemplate the lowly destiny, some Homer should sing the saga, of the mule and of his place in the South." Otherwise, except for very slight differences in punctuation, the lines quoted are identical with those in *Sartoris* (Signet ed.), 226.

nerese," though this mule anticipates certain traits of Faulkner's archetypal bear, as memorable in turn as Melville's whale. But the voice—this uninhibited expression of a strange temperament, this love of verbal play—is that of a writer fully assured of his own powers.

It is interesting to listen, in a great writer's earliest work, for the first faint tonalities of a still undiscovered "mature" voice; and also to be on the watch for hints of later obsession. The second sentence of *Soldiers' Pay* is remarkably Faulknerian, even to the ironic parenthetical aside: "He suffered the same jaundice that many a more booted one than he did, from Flight Commanders through Generals to the ambrosial single-barred (not to mention that inexplicable beast of the field which the French so beautifully call an aspiring aviator); they had stopped the war on him." [6]

But much of *Soldiers' Pay* only reminds us that Faulkner was a derivative poet *manqué,* with a *fin de siècle* clever prettiness: "Beyond the oaks, against a wall of poplars in a restless row were columns of a Greek temple, yet the poplars themselves in slim vague green were poised and vain as girls in a frieze. Against a privet hedge would soon be lilies like nuns in a cloister and blue hyacinths swung soundless bells, dreaming of Lesbos." [7] For a seminar I once pedantically catalogued the image clusters of *Soldiers' Pay*: silver associated with beautiful trees, with dream, with stricken poplar, with arrested or carven water, with frieze; and these with the girl Cecily. I suspect Faulkner thought he despised the disloyal, cowardly, and epicene Cecily. But the imagery suggests he was attracted more than he realized by her. The frieze image of life eternally arrested, Keats's Grecian urn, will become a favorite one.

A long-unpublished story or sketch called "Nympholepsy" is

---

[6]Signet ed., 7.
[7]*Ibid.*, 43.

even more instructive. It was apparently written in the first month or two after Faulkner's arrival in New Orleans, in 1925, and is an expansion of a sketch called "The Hill," published in *The Mississippian*, the undergraduate newspaper, in 1922.[8] It immediately precedes the writing of *Soldiers' Pay* and is certainly more interesting, more revealing than the published New Orleans sketches. The first sentences strikingly anticipate Quentin Compson's concern with his shadow: "Soon the sharp line of the hill-crest had cut off his shadow's head; and pushing it like a snake before him he saw it gradually become nothing. At last he had no shadow at all." The third sentence has a rather lovely image ("dust was like a benediction upon him, and upon the day of labor behind him"), though the loveliness is Conrad's. After the *Patna*'s hot days on "the great blaze of the ocean," the "nights descended on her like a benediction." It is altogether normal, even proper, that a young writer should echo a loved master. What is still more promising is audacity, even absurd audacity. I was delighted as well as outraged, in the late 1930s, when I came upon this in *Mosquitoes*: "Twilight ran in like a quiet violet dog." But the dog of "Nympholepsy" is even more startling: "The sun was a red descending furnace mouth, his shadow he had thought lost crouched like a skulking dog at his feet."

The sketch tries out some of *Soldiers' Pay*'s decadent poetry. "From here the court-house was a dream dreamed by Thucydides: you could not see that pale Ionic columns were stained with casual tobacco." Or, "Below him a barn took the moon for a silver edge and a silo became a dream dreamed in Greece, apple trees broke into silver like gesturing fountains." Tree branches are "like the hands of misers reluctantly dripping golden coins of sunset." But there are also a few moments of more characteristic

---

[8]"The Hill" is totally devoid of the sexual anxiety of "Nympholepsy," or of any real sexual content. Reprinted in Carvel Collins (ed.), *William Faulkner: Early Prose and Poetry* (Boston, 1962), 90–92.

Faulknerian audacity. Brittle corn stalks hinder the speed of a running man "with wanton and static unconcern." "Still running, he crossed the wheat slumbrous along the moony land"; standing grain is of "dull and unravished gold." A decidedly anxious sexual fantasy anticipates Ike's logistic difficulties with his Olympian cow: rotten bark slipping under his feet; the elusive female swinging herself dripping up the bank. "His heavy water-soaked clothes clung to him like importunate sirens, like women." *Post coitum animal triste.*

The major interest of "Nympholepsy" is in fact psychological; it is the most explicit and unrepressed expression of the misogyny or sexual anxiety that will provide an important undercurrent in some of the later work. Once again the resemblances with the very early Conrad, who was no less misogynous, are startling. A menace in Conrad's unfinished *The Sisters* of 1896 is of "grass unconquerable . . . vanquishing the slender trees," but elsewhere the trees themselves are menacing, and the landscape of "The Lagoon" is altogether paranoid. In "Nympholepsy" the trees are "calm and uncaring as gods, and the remote sky" is "like a silken pall to hide his unsightly dissolution." "These trees gazed on him impersonally, taking a slow revenge." "Before this green cathedral of trees he stood for a while, empty as a sheep, feeling the dying day draining from the world as a bath-tub drains, or a cracked bowl; and he could hear the day repeating slow orisons in a green nave."

This is incomparably absurd. But the important literary fact, the promising fact, is that Faulkner did not repress his sexual fantasy or suppress his verbal audacity. The cause of all this anxiety is a girl or woman, perhaps nonexistent, glimpsed at a distance. "Then his once-clean instincts become swinish got him lurching into motion." For the "desire for a woman's body" has "the purpose of seducing him from the avenues of safety, of security where others of his kind ate and slept." The sexual prohibition has, moreover, vague religious overtones. "That sensation of an imminent displeasure and anger, of a Being whom he had offended, he held away from himself. But it still hung like poised wings about and above him." The actual menace is of water on which no "boat would swim"; "he awaited abrupt and dreadful annihilation." He is aware of the deity, the "imminent Presence," even as he seems about to slip into the water, about to die. Then the water took him, anticipating several of the painful sexual encounters of the later fiction:

Then the water took him. But here was something more than water. The water ran darkly between his body and his overalls and shirt, he felt his hair lap backward wetly. But here beneath his hand a startled thigh slid like a snake, among dark bubbles he felt a swift leg; and, sinking, the point of a breast scraped his back. Amid a slow commotion of disturbed water he saw death like a woman shining and drowned and waiting, saw a flashing body tortured by water; and his lungs spewing water gulped wet air.[9]

A slightly later fragment turned up in 1970 in a closet at Rowan Oak, "And Now What's To Do." Here the sexual dread is not even displaced onto a fantasied water nymph whose breasts scrape. Girls are

Soft things. Secretive, but like traps. Like going after something you wanted, and getting into a nest of spider webs. You got the thing, then you had to pick the webs off, and every time you touched one, it stuck to you. Even after you didn't want the thing anymore, the webs clung to you. Until after a while you remembered the way the webs itched and you wanted the thing again, just thinking of how the webs itched. No. Quicksand. That was it. Wade through once, then go on. But a man wont. He wants to go all the way through, somehow; break out on the other side. Everything incomplete somehow. Having to back off, with webs clinging to you.[10]

---

[9]James B. Meriwether (ed.), *A Faulkner Miscellany* (Jackson, Miss., 1974), 153. Joseph Blotner summarizes unexcitedly: "Having glimpsed a girl in the failing light, he played faun to her nymph. Giving chase unsuccessfully, he narrowly escaped drowning in a stream." *Faulkner: A Biography* (New York, 1974), I, 414.

[10]Meriwether (ed.), *A Faulkner Miscellany*, 147.

The Faulknerian Voice

No doubt the misogyny (and of course I am referring to the writer and his inmost temperament, not to the man with a perhaps normally active romantic and erotic life) represents a limitation in the imaginative and moral equipment of a very great writer.[11] But it did, consciously indulged, give strength and structure to *Sanctuary,* and lent bite to a number of superb vignettes—the bony, angular Charlotte Rittenmeyer and the Tall Convict's swollen passenger, and Laverne sexually assaulting the pilot in midair, and Mink Snopes's insatiable wife, perhaps even the bovine child Eula Varner and her mammalian ellipses, not yet the rather boring regenerated heroine. We would be the poorer without these frightening ladies. But what I want to insist on, for this very early work, is the relative freedom from inhibition and repression. In *Mosquitoes* Faulkner could treat incest playfully, with *fellatio* displaced onto the sisterly biting of an ear; or, a whisper of his later humorous voice, could speak of a possibly drowned guest in terms of "floating inert buttocks in some lonely reach of the lake, that would later wash ashore with that mute inopportune implacability of the drowned."

Faulkner would in time show himself exceptionally receptive to whatever—in terms of verbal surprise or startling analogy— fantasy and the unconscious proposed. This willingness to "let go," to take risks, to keep the avenues from the unconscious open, to be absurd—these were necessary to the great developments of the 1930s. As Conrad had to write "The Lagoon," so Faulkner had to write "Nympholepsy."

It was necessary to learn and know that, given language

---

[11]The exceedingly complex question of the relationship of "real-life" sexual feelings to those that appear, often inadvertently, in imaginative works cannot be dismissed in a sentence. A psychobiography of Faulkner remains to be written. For the misogyny and sexual anxiety evident in the fiction, see my *The Triumph of the Novel: Dickens, Dostoevsky, Faulkner* (New York, 1976), 109–35.

powerful enough, readers might be made to believe anything, even Ike McCaslin raising his hand in salute to a rattlesnake and addressing him in the old tongue as Chief and Grandfather: " 'the old one, the ancient and accursed about the earth, fatal and solitary and he could smell it now: the thin sick smell of rotting cucumbers and something else which had no name, evocative of all knowledge and an old weariness and of pariah-hood and of death.' " Or believe Old Ben, "not even a mortal beast but an anachronism indomitable and invincible out of an old dead time, a phantom, epitome and apotheosis of the old wild life which the little puny humans swarmed and hacked at in a fury of abhorrence and fear like pygmies about the ankles of a drowsing elephant;—the old bear, solitary, indomitable, and alone; widowered childless and absolved of mortality—old Priam reft of his old wife and outlived all his sons."

There are many variants of the Faulknerian voice, even uneccentric variants where only a strange word or two, a surprising perverse turn of thought, identifies the author. Faulkner is capable of anything: the spare reporting of "That Evening Sun" and "A Rose for Emily"; the varied interior monologues of *As I Lay Dying*; the Flaubertian polish and controlled ironic denigrations of *Sanctuary*; the moving un-adorned notation of Wilbourne's thoughts as he elects forty years' grief over nothing, grinding the saving poison into the floor, and looks out at the concrete hulk where a life of poverty, but still life, goes on; or the beautifully modulated comic palinodes and dying closes of *The Sound and the Fury, Light in August* and *The Hamlet,* and of *The Town* with its appealingly savage Indian Snopes children. Faulkner is even a master of realistic dialogue when he wishes to be: Wash Jones's "Air you Rosie Coldfield? Then you better come on out yon. Henry has done shot that durn French feller. Kilt him dead as a beef." Or Miss Rosa in her less Shakespearean moments:

"You nigger! What's your name?"

"Calls me Jim Bond."

"Help me up. You aint any Sutpen! You dont have to leave me lying in the dirt!"

Criticism has perhaps taken such traditional expertise too much for granted. And it has ignored or noticed only in passing the experiments that are derivative, but brilliantly derivative—the Joycean stream of consciousness of *Mosquitoes* and the Joycean doublets and coinages of *Pylon*: the traffic of Grandlieu Street "rushing in a light curbchanneled spindrift of tortured and draggled serpentine and trodden confetti pending the dawn's white-wings—spent tinseldung of Momus' Nilebarge clatterfalque." We detect a truer Faulknerian voice later in *Pylon*, as Laverne, as it happens wearing no underpants, descends by parachute toward a sexually fascinated police officer. For this Faulkner is playful, is playing with both male and female depravity, and playing simultaneously with syntax and diction. The officer "besotted and satiated by his triumphs over abased human flesh which his corrupt and picayune office supplied him, seeing now and without forewarning the ultimate shape of his jaded desires fall upon him out of the sky, not merely naked but clothed in the very traditional symbology—the ruined dress with which she was trying wildly to cover her loins, and the parachute harness—of female bondage." [12] *Besotted, satiated, abased, corrupt, picayune*: five strongly "loaded" words out of fifteen. A very Faulknerian device this, to dip so swiftly and tellingly down from the general elevation his prose sustains. "The prolonged hovering flight of the subjective over the outstretched ground of the case exposed," James wrote of Conrad's method. These sudden vicious descents from the hovering are more frequent in Faulkner.

---

[12]Modern Library ed., 196–97.

Let me acknowledge a final time that Faulkner can write straight, traditional prose as beautiful as any in our language. But what is more characteristic and recognizable is extravagant "Faulknerese," a term I use with allusion to Conrad's own description of some of his lush early prose as "Conradese." A name that also immediately occurs is Shakespeare's, since the linguistic convention in several of the novels (but most obviously in *Absalom, Absalom!*) is that of Shakespearean blank verse. The major characters in moments of intense feeling all speak in a "not-language" arbitrarily elevated above that of realistic prose discourse of this or any other century—a language more rapid yet more involuted in rhythm, more eccentric in syntax, more elaborate and more abstract in diction, infinitely more metaphorical. At the italicized extreme of Miss Rosa's long discourse I think we are to assume that the words are not actually spoken aloud; that we are listening instead to what her most inward tortured spirit would ideally like to say: the *"prisoner soul, miasmal-distillant"* that *"wroils ever upward sunward, tugs its tenous prisoner arteries and veins."* The complication of syntax and meaning is Shakespearean; so too the conversion of parts of speech; so too the large metaphors of the body and the games of legalism and logic. Miss Rosa's voice has its affinities with Shreve's sardonic one, " 'That this Faustus, this demon, this Beelzebub fled hiding from some momentary flashy glare of his Creditor's outraged face exasperated beyond all endurance, hiding, scuttling into respectability like a jackal into a rockpile, so she thought at first, until she realized that he was not hiding, did not want to hide, was merely engaged in one final frenzy of evil and harm-doing before the Creditor overtook him next time for good and all.' " [13] This is very close to Quentin's, italicized at this point in the novel, *"and the aunt twelve miles away watching from her distance as the two*

---

[13]*Absalom, Absalom!* (Modern Library ed.), 178.

daughters watched from theirs the old demon, the ancient varicose and despairing Faustus fling his final main now with the Creditor's hand already on his shoulder . . ." [14] which is not too distant from Mr. Compson reflecting on Charles Bon, " 'the man reclining in a flowered, almost feminized gown, in a sunny window in his chambers—this man handsome elegant and even catlike and too old to be where he was, too old not in years but in experience, with some tangible effluvium of knowledge, surfeit: of actions done and satiations plumbed and pleasures exhausted and even forgotten.' " [15] And no prose, no voice is more Faulknerian than that of Charles Bon's wartime letter written in stove polish: *"it is only the mind, the gross omnivorous carrion-heavy soul which becomes inured; the body itself, thank God, never reconciled from the old soft feel of soap and clean linen and something between the sole of the foot and the earth to distinguish it from the foot of a beast."* [16]

All these voices are closely related to the frankly authorial voice of the novel's first two pages. It is important to note (however appalled we may be by elaboration) two things that are also true of Shakespeare's plays. First, these *are* voices. Even the most outrageously recondite analogies and abstractions are spoken as by living human beings, not "merely written" by a well-fed but soulless computer. Second, there is as much variation among these voices as in the most faithfully drab realistic fiction—Miss Rosa's voice as different from Quentin's as his from Charles Bon's, and more different, among them, than the standard personages of, say, John Cheever. (Here however it is well to acknowledge how exceedingly close Quentin's voice can be to Shreve McCannon's, or Ike McCaslin's to McCaslin Edmonds's voice in *The Bear*. In these instances, but in *The Bear* especially, the dialogue approximates interior discourse.

---

[14]*Ibid.*, 182.
[15]*Ibid.*, 95.
[16]*Ibid.*, 130.

There are times when, psychologically speaking, Quentin and Ike are debating with more skeptical selves.)

I would like, finally, to restate a distinction made briefly in *The Triumph of the Novel* between two major variants of the fully liberated or fully realized Faulknerian voice—the voice already moderately free in "The Bear," in long rolling paragraphs of "Old Man," in *Absalom, Absalom!* and *The Hamlet*, and splendidly, outrageously in the best pages of *Requiem for a Nun* and *A Fable*.

I termed the first variant Jamesian: recalling, that is, the involuted, logic-chopping, parenthetical, almost crazily qualifying mentality of Henry James, the later James of course, for whom a straightforward simple statement had become impossible. The prose is that of thinking that is both nervous and ironic, and that takes frank delight in the play of logic and syntax; delight, too, in verbal structure and in sudden breaks in consciousness. It is a cinema of the mind fascinated by its own operation. I quote some 385 words of a 3000-word passage; all but 400 of the 3000 are digressive. The context is a courthouse scene, with a lawyer hoping, through rhetoric, to deter mob action long enough for a prisoner to escape. The lawyer is compared to a bullfighter, as well as to the old pagan splashing the hearth ritually, "in recognition of them who had matched him with his hour upon the earth"; he decides to speak. There is a long disquisition on a painting which he claims "to have bought for the sole purpose of not having to pretend that he liked it." The passage perhaps says that heroic opportunity, like aesthetic experience, is gratuitous. It exhibits, in any event, the purest Faulknerian perversity, a voice that is truly his own, yet a voice sufficiently linked to that of James to make the Old Pretender stir, if only briefly, in his New England grave:

So the lawyer could have stopped now, with one word leaving them once more fixed, as with one twitch of his cape the espada does the bull, and walk again through the door to the judge's chambers and on to the hotel and pack and strap his bag. But he did not: who owed this little more, as the old pagan, before he quaffed it empty, tilted always from the goblet's brimming rim one splash at least upon the hearth not to placate but simply in recognition of them who had matched him with his hour upon the earth; in one of the houses on one of the best streets in one of the most unassailable sections of New Orleans, he owned a picture, a painting, no copy but proved genuine and coveted, for which he had paid more than he liked to remember even though it had been validated by experts before he bought it and revalidated twice since and for which he had been twice offered half again what he had paid for it, and which he had not liked then and still didn't and was not even certain he knew what it meant, but which—so he believed then, with more truth than any save himself knew—he affirmed to have bought for the sole purpose of not having to pretend that he liked it; one evening, alone in his study (wifeless and childless, in the house too save for the white-jacketed soft-footed not tamed but merely tractable mulatto murderer) suddenly he found himself looking at no static rectangle of disturbing Mediterranean blues and saffrons and ochres, not even at the signboard affirming like a trumpet-blast the inevictable establishment in coeval space of the sun of his past—[17]

in the copying of which I, on July 22, 1977, was suddenly translated back in total Proustian recall to a dusty classroom of approximately 1928, and the nightmare of diagramming sentences on a blackboard; and so thankful that A *Fable* had not yet been published or for that matter any Faulkner yet swum into my teacher's ken.

The second variant I call Miltonic. I think I first called it that out of sheer perversity, to bedevil a distinguished Milton scholar who didn't have much use for Faulkner. And yet Miltonic is the right word—a Miltonic love of lyrical extravagance and running rhythms, with a conscious, outrageously indulged pleasure in extended simile and esoteric allusion, essentially a liberated flight of mind over time and space, in which divers myths and cultures are absurdly and beautifully juxtaposed, as so often in

---

[17]First hardback ed., 183; Signet ed., 172–73.

Paradise Lost. Here too we have dizzying involution and logic; we have widely diverse elements grouped into triads and pairs; we have the suspended periodic inversions of syntax. The occasion here is the remark that "Rapacity does not fail, else man must deny he breathes." This provokes a Miltonic survey of civilization:

Civilization itself is its password and Christianity its masterpiece; Chartres and the Sistine chapel, the pyramids and the rock-wombed powder-magazines under the gates of Hercules its altars and monuments, Michelangelo and Phidias and Newton and Ericsson and Archimedes and Krupp its priests and popes and bishops; the long deathless roster of its glory—Caesar and the Barcas and the two Macedonians, our own Bonaparte and the great Russian and the giants who strode nimbused in red hair like fire across the Aurora Borealis, and all the lesser nameless who were not heroes but, glorious in anonymity, at least served the destiny of heroes—the generals and admirals, the corporals and ratings of glory, the batmen and orderlies of renown, and the chairmen of boards and the presidents of federations, the doctors and lawyers and educators and churchmen who after nineteen centuries have rescued the son of heaven from oblivion and translated him from mere meek heir to earth to chairman of its board of trade; and those who did not even have names and designations to be anonymous from—the hands and the backs which carved and sweated aloft the stone blocks and painted the ceilings and invented the printing presses and grooved the barrels, down to the last indestructible voice which asked nothing but the right to speak of hope in Roman lion-pits and murmur the name of God from the Indian-anticked pyres in Canadian forests—stretching immutable and enduring further back than man's simple remembering recorded it. Not rapacity: it does not fail; suppose Mithridates' and Heliogabalus' heir had used his heritage in order to escape his inheritees: Mithridates and Heliogabalus were Heliogabalus and Mithridates still and that scurry from Oran was still only a mouse's, since one of Grimalkin's parents was patience too and that whole St. Cyr-Toulon-Africa business merely flight, as when the maiden flees the ravisher not toward sanctuary but privacy, and just enough of it to make the victory memorable and its trophy a prize.[18]

---

[18]First hardback ed., 259–60; Signet ed., 235–36.

The Faulknerian Voice

Is even "Miltonic" an adequate epithet for this richly intoxicated flow of language and history? The long view of history, in which all heroes and all victims become contemporary, is Miltonic. But Faulkner's long view is also more compassionate than Milton's, more aware of those "glorious in anonymity." And the passage ends in logical complications more perverse than those with which Milton torments our students. The rythmic balancing of clauses, the pyramidal as well as periodic sentences, the punctuation or absence of punctuation that compels the reader to chant, the incessant verbal surprises—all these suggest, as *primum mobile* of the Faulknerian voice, unregenerate love of language, of games, of intellectual play: the lovely, absurd, humane comedy of mind.

Sex & History: Origins of Faulkner's Apocrypha

LEWIS P. SIMPSON

As defined by the distinguished British historian R. W. Southern, the stages of the historian's experience of history are as follows: "first the individual perceptions which are the bricks out of which our historical edifices are built; then the ramifications of these perceptions to every area of social or private life to form large areas of intelligibility; and finally the arranging of this material to form works of art of a special and distinctive kind." [1] Reading Professor Southern's analysis of the historical experience at a moment when I was thinking about the great historical construct Faulkner wrought out of his literary art, the tales of Yoknapatawpha (and thinking too about how often Faulkner compared his work as a novelist to that of the carpenter), I found myself asking if the pattern of the historian's experience of history as set forth by Southern would fit Faulkner's experience of history. The question I was asking being in totality far too large to be taken up in the project immediately before me—that of exploring further the subject of sex and history in relation to the origins of Yoknapatawpha[2]—I turned to Professor Southern's

---

[1]R.W. Southern, "The Historical Experience," *Times Literary Supplement*, June 24, 1977, p. 771.
[2]See Lewis P. Simpson, "Faulkner and the Legend of the Artist," in *Faulkner: Fifty Years After The Marble Faun*, ed. George H. Wolfe (Tuscaloosa: University of Alabama Press, 1976).

prescription for his own lecture: "But here I shall examine only the first and most primitive stage of all—the sources and characteristics of the initial perceptions." I impose this prescription as my own here, and ask only this: if one tries to adapt Southern's formula of the historical experience to Faulkner, what does one set down as the record of the initial, or primitive, stage?

Professor Southern characterizes this initial stage as that in which the historian confronting a chaos of information glimpses a "small area of intelligibility." [3] Of course a novelist—although all novelists are historians—does not work by accumulating information, hoping to put it together in such a manner as to deduce significant meaning from it. The early task of the novelist is more awesome. Unless he is a truncated novelist who limits himself to writing colorful fictions about certain historical periods and so is hardly a novelist at all, the novelist seeks to perceive areas of intelligibility in the raw history of the streets and rooms he lives in or enters—of the areas of human activity he knows, being born into them or coming into them in the course of living. The novelist from the beginning of his career has an impulsion to a greater intimacy with history than the historian proper. This may be more true if, like Faulkner, the novelist in his early stage of development goes through a period when he tries to be a poet. In this effort he intensifies his concern with language—with individual words—for poems live almost solely in the preciseness of their cultural evocation. While Faulkner was not a markedly successful poet, and recognized this before he had written very many poems, he did publish two volumes of poetry and always attached considerable significance to his having tried his hand at making poems. He did so with justification, for it is in the poems that the initial stage of his perception, or experience of history, is defined. More than foreshadowed in them, it is in effect formulated in

---

[3]Southern, "The Historical Experience," 771.

their attempt to express with poetic precision the fundamental connection of sex and history. To see how this is so illuminates the essential inception (before any one of them was written) of the emotional—let me say, spiritual—character of the series of fictions set in Yoknapatawpha, which Faulkner came to call, in more than a nominal sense, "my apocryphal county." [4]

Perhaps I can get most directly into the early perception of the nexus of sex and history in Faulkner by referring to one of his irregular Italian sonnets. Written before 1925, possibly in 1924, this poem is numbered XLII in *A Green Bough*. (Although not published until 1933, this volume collects poems written during Faulkner's poetic period several years earlier.) The octave of the sonnet (rhymed in the Shakespearean rather than the Italian style) interprets the symbolism of the story of the Hebraic Garden of Eden in a literal way.

> Beneath the apple tree Eve's tortured shape
> Glittered in the Snake's, her riven breast
> Sloped his coils and took the sun's escape
> To augur black her sin from east to west.
> In winter's night man may keep him warm
> Regretting olden sins he did omit;
> With fetiches the whip of blood to charm,
> Forgetting that with breath he's heir to it.

The sestet expands and comments on the theme of the octave— the seduction of Eve by Satan and the consequent repression of the instinctive desires of the blood—as follows:

> But old gods fall away, the ancient Snake
> Is throned and crowned instead, and has for minion
> That golden apple which will never slake

---

[4]For instances of the use of the term see Faulkner to Harold Ober, January 5, 1946, February 1, 1948, in Joseph Blotner (ed.), *Selected Letters of William Faulkner* (New York: Random House, 1977), 218, 262.

But ever feed man's crumb of fire, when plover
And swallow and shrill northing birds whip over
Nazarene and Roman and Virginian.[5]

The defeat of the old gods of the Greco-Roman mythology and
the enthronement of the power of the Hebraic snake, the power
of the knowledge of good and evil, paradoxically does not
suppress man's cosmic "crumb of fire" but, opposing it, feeds it.
Flaring up when the birds go north in the spring to nest and to
renew life, it whips "over Nazarene and Roman and Virginian."
That is, it wields the "whip of blood" over the dominion of
Christian history. Faulkner's imagery is clumsy and its implication obvious: under the dominion of the Hebraic snake,
man becomes a self-conscious sexual creature and a self-
conscious historical being. A less obvious implication is that in
the seduction of Eve every sexual act, like every act of man,
becomes a historical act. At the time he had his vision of Eve's
tortured shape beneath the apple tree, I doubt that Faulkner
quite understood its more subtle implication. Probably he never
did in a sharp, rational way—not, I should say, because he was
incapable of such perception but because he was never entirely
reconciled to Eve's seduction. His irreconciliation created in his
vision of Yoknapatawpha a myriad tension between the cosmological and historical modes of existence.

Yet I do not intend to say that Faulkner opposed the cosmological to the historical. I mean that his perception of history
found a focus in the tension generated in the literary imagination
by the conquest of the cosmic sexuality of the Greco-Roman
garden by the historicism of the Hebraic-Christian interpretation of sexuality. In his response to this tension is to be discovered Faulkner's shaping experience of history.

But I am getting ahead of the story. The earliest stage of

---

[5]*A Green Bough* (New York: Harrison Smith and Robert Haas, 1933), 65.

46

Faulkner's historical perception is a vision simpler than that of
the historicism of Hebraic-Christian sexuality. It is simply a
vision of the world grown old, a world which has lost the vitality
of cosmic unity. The theme of the aging world is graphically
present in a nine-line poem in *The Green Bough* (number
XXVI), in which the withdrawal of the moon goddess is the
subject.

> Still, and look down, look down:
> Thy curious withdrawn hand
> Unprobes, now spirit and sense unblend, undrown,
> Knit by a word and sundered by a tense
> Like this: Is: Was: and Not. Nor caught between
> Spent beaches and the annealed insatiate sea
> Dost myriad lie, cold and intact Selene,
> On secret strange or old disastrous lee
> Behind the fading mistral of the sense.[6]

In this short poem, possibly the best poem Faulkner ever wrote,
the austere behavior of Selene, the moon goddess, is associated
with the modern rupture of sense and spirit. It is an effective
symbol of the estrangement from the world which occurs as,
becoming a part of the historical consciousness, the world ceases
to be a cosmos.

In Faulkner's first book of poems (and in his first published
book, *The Marble Faun*, 1924), the aging of the world is the
predominant theme. In fact the world has grown so old there is
virtually no sexual activity. Both the Faun imprisoned in his
"marble bonds" and dreaming of pastoral freedom and the Pan
who appears in his dreaming are chaste creatures. The Faun
sees but does not pursue the golden nymphs. Pan, far from
being the "goat god," is present in the voice of his pipe, invoking
a beautiful but strangely empty Arcadia. Yet in spite of its sexual

[6]*Ibid.*, 48.

passivity, *The Marble Faun* displays a certain tension between the Faun's recollection of the cosmic garden and a sense of the Edenic garden. In the Prologue, the Faun complains that he cannot break his "marble bonds" yet "That quick keen snake / Is free to come and go." In a later passage the Faun, hearing the pipes of Pan, glides "like a snake" to "peer" into the "leafy depths" where Pan sits on "a chill rock gray and old" as he had "since the world began." [7] The triumphant snake is present, it would seem, in the gray garden of the Faun's imprisonment. Locked in the statue in the garden, the Faun is a creature of his consciousness of art and history. He imagines his situation, so to speak, as an experience of history.

In general, Faulkner's poems—and for that matter several of the prose sketches he wrote in his youth—indicate clearly that the earliest stage of his perception of history occurs in his experience of the world alienation, which (under the rubrics of romanticism, impressionism, surrealism, etc.) dominates the mood and subject matter of modern literature and art. In spite of the fact that in his youth Faulkner's literary attitudes reek of Edwardian decadence, his early sensibility cannot be dismissed as merely imitative. Seeking the displaced connection between sense and spirit, the young Faulkner was fascinated by the drama of "Is, Was, and Not." Whether or not Selene might return her hand to the world was no mere idle dream of an imagination stuffed with the poems of Swinburne and old numbers of the *Yellow Book*. Faulkner early made a heavy emotional investment in Arcadia and in all the beings who populated the Greco-Roman imagination of the cosmos. From first to last these mythical beings are present in his writings. At times visible, at times invisible, they are always there. But they are never invoked by Faulkner's imagination as pure cosmic presences. Not even in the earliest writings does Faulkner have

---

[7]*The Marble Faun* (Boston: The Four Seas Company, 1924), 12, 16.

the illusion that Arcadia still exists in the human consciousness; save, that is, as illusion.

In the poetic schema suggested in Faulkner's poems, Arcadia became a part of the historical consciousness when the Western imagination transformed the cosmological garden into the Garden of Eden; when Satan entered the garden, seduced Eve, and forever sundered sense and spirit in the self-conscious act of sexuality. As the first poem I have referred to says, the old gods fell away. Pan was transformed into Satan, and the rest is history. Faulkner, in other words—in what may be termed the second stage of his historical experience—perceived the historicizing of sexuality as the key element in the differentiation of the human consciousness of existence in a historical society from existence in the organic, or compact—the undifferentiated—society. Equating the differentiation of self-conscious sexuality and the differentiation of history (although surely with no deliberate knowledge that he was doing this), Faulkner in his initial writings entered into the literary and artistic experience of world historical alienation. And like all the great modern writers, including Joyce, Eliot, and Mann, he took this as his subject. The development of Faulkner's own version of the modern estrangement and the making of this into his novelistic substance is the third stage of his primary historical experience.

In this stage Faulkner discovered a symbol of alienation in the difficulty the modern historical consciousness has in responding to sexuality and began with increasing complexity to employ specific sexual situations as emblems of the estrangement of modern consciousness from a unified or harmonious order of sense and spirit. I will pass over the interesting foreshadowing of this kind of symbolization in Faulkner's little poetic drama, *Marionettes* (1920),[8] and remark on it in his first two novels,

---

[8]See Noel Polk, "William Faulkner's *Marionettes*," in *A Faulkner Miscellany*, ed. James B. Meriwether (Jackson: University Press of Mississippi, 1974), 3–36.

Soldiers' Pay and *Mosquitoes,* and in the inaugural works of the Yoknapatawpha series: the fragment called *Father Abraham, Flags in the Dust* (published as *Sartoris*), and *The Sound and the Fury.*

A story set in a small town in Georgia right after the First World War, *Soldiers' Pay* has varied facets, but it is not misleading to emphasize the theme of sexual frustration. The novel is fundamentally about the defeat of the spirit of wonder and of desire, of the poetry of living, by modern history. Donald Mahon, an American aviator shot down over Flanders and lying in a comatose state in the home of his father, an Episcopal priest and rector, is not only a type of the poet but a faun returned into history. Swimming naked in the creek with the pretty servant girl Emmy, running with her in the night, and making love to her, he has converted her into a nymph. Januarius Jones, a fat and repulsive satyr returned into history, corrupts Emmy. A ridiculous figure yet a sinister force of lust, Januarius is the most strongly conceived character in the novel. The element of fantasy in his makeup is more sucessfully assimilated to his reality as a creature of history than it is in the cases of Donald and Emmy. All three characters are aspects of the great god Pan, who returns, or tries to return, into a world in which he is as dead as Christ is.[9] The reiteration of the motif of "sex and death and damnation" in *Soldiers' Pay* provides for the feeling of a dead-end historical situation. Falling within the ambiance of the waste land as projected by Eliot, *Soldiers' Pay* proclaims the damnation attendant upon the triumph of a pervasive "ennui" in the aftermath of the First World War and the general victory of an industrialized and spiritually trivialized society.[10] There is a

---

[9]Many aspects of the Pan-Christ identification are discussed in Patricia Merivale, *Pan the Goat-God: His Myth in Modern Times* (Cambridge: Harvard University Press, 1969), 14–16 *passim.*

[10]The sense of "ennui" is an implied motif in both *Soliders' Pay* and *Mosquitoes.* A major study of the motif in Western culture is provided in Reinhard Kuhn, *The Demon of Noontide: Ennui in Western Literature* (Princeton: Princeton University Press, 1976).

suggestion, however—and I think this may be the most significant part of *Soldiers' Pay*—of an association between the
generalized historical situation and its relation to the historical
situation in the American South. This occurs in a description of
the courthouse square of Charlestown, Georgia. The depiction
of the somnolent scene of southern apathy is climaxed by an
effusive image: "And above all brooded early April sweetly
pregnant with noon." [11] Ridiculous as it is, the image declares
an increasing boldness in Faulkner's imagination. By the time he
wrote *Soldiers' Pay* he was trying for an ironic juxtaposition of
historical actuality and pastoral sexuality that he had not before
attempted. He not only brings the pastoral deities back to the
rose garden of the Reverend Mr. Mahon but into a courthouse
square in Georgia. Soon this would be the square in Jefferson, Yoknapatawpha County, Mississippi. Across the Jefferson
square would walk avatars of the gods, goddesses, and minor
deities of the lost Arcadia who are among the most memorable
characters in American novelistic literature.

But Faulkner's perception of the complex fate of creatures
from the pastoral cosmos who return into modern history had
yet to be refined or even substantially developed. In his second
novel, *Mosquitoes*, he is no longer interested in the more or less
literal return of fleet fauns, virginal nymphs, and wanton satyrs
consumed with nympholepsy. He creates more subtle avatars of
the pastoral figures, especially in the nymphlike Pat Robyn, and,
more especially, in the sculptor Gordon. Gordon is a tall,
angular man with a hawk face (in the moonlight a "silver faun's
face") and a dark-bearded head (something like a Laurence
Housman version of Pan in the *Yellow Book*). He is a full-fledged
yet elusive suggestion of the modern artist as avatar of Pan. But
Faulkner also identifies Gordon with the Christian myth of
history, precisely with Christ and the Passion Week. In so

---

[11]*Soldiers' Pay* (New York: Liveright Publishing Company, 1954), 112.

doing, Faulkner rather forcibly but with some success unites concepts of the sexuality of art and the sexuality of history. He accomplishes this primarily by means of two symbols. One is a representation of a female figure in marble which Gordon has done and which he greatly prizes.

> As you entered the room the thing drew your eyes: you turned sharply as to a sound, expecting movement. But it was marble, it could not move. And when you tore your eyes away and turned your back on it at last, you got again untarnished and high and clean that sense of swiftness, of space encompassed; but on looking again it was as before: motionless and passionately eternal—the virginal breastless torso of a girl, headless, armless, legless, in marble temporarily caught and hushed yet passionate still for escape, passionate and simple and eternal in the equivocal derisive darkness of the world. Nothing to trouble your youth or lack of it: rather something to trouble the very fibrous integrity of your being.[12]

The other symbol is a clay mask of Mrs. Maurier, the patron of New Orleans writers, artists, and intellectuals. Her invitation to a mixed bag of them to spend a week aboard her yacht, the *Nausikka*, provides what little plot *Mosquitoes* has, the record of an aborted odyssey on Lake Pontchartrain.

> It was clay, yet damp, and from out its dull, dead grayness Mrs. Maurier looked at them. Her chins, harshly, and her flaccid jaw muscles with savage versimilitude. Her eyes were caverns thumbed with two motions into the dead familiar astonishment of her face; and yet, behind them, somewhere within those empty sockets, behind all her familiar surprise, there was something else—something that exposed her face for the mask it was, and still more, a mask unaware.[13]

The marble abstraction of the female body represents a passionate erotic grief in Gordon's life that is never revealed beyond hints given in the rhetoric of a second-rate Cyrano de Bergerac. Nonetheless the highly wrought and perfected vir-

---

[12]*Mosquitoes* (New York: Liveright Publishing Company, 1955), 152, 11.
[13]*Ibid.*, 322.

ginal torso is the source of the perception of the mask, and still
more, the mask unaware which is Mrs. Maurier's face. Gordon's
exploration of the depths of the personal consciousness has given
him the power (suggested to Faulkner by Bergson)[14] to intuit
human experience in its historical fullness and actuality.

Faulkner reinforces the point by having the Semitic man, a
figure of the literary intellectual in *Mosquitoes*, tell the story of
Mrs. Maurier. It is a story involving the unwilling marriage of a
New England girl to a much older man, who during the Civil
War had disappeared from the plantation where he was an
overseer. After the end of hostilities he turned up astride a
Union cavalry saddle and with a hundred thousand dollars in
uncut federal notes in his possession. Forced by her parents to
desert her true love for a marriage of convenience to this
nouveau addition to the southern gentry, Mrs. Maurier has long
outlived her husband. Yet as the Semitic man sees and Gordon
has discerned, this aging childless widow is yet alive to life.
What Gordon has caught in her mask is fundamentally the thing
he has caught in the marble abstraction of the young girl, the
mystique of virginity and desire and the grief of unfulfillment. At
first, the Semitic man says, you may think that Mrs. Maurier's
penchant for collecting writers and artists is "just silliness, lack
of occupation—a tub of washing, to be exact." But he says he has
come to "see something thwarted back of it all, something
stifled, yet which won't quite die." Dawson Fairchild, a novelist
who is listening intently to the Semitic man's divination, exclaims, "A virgin. . . . That's what it is, exactly. Fooling with
sex, kind of dabbling at it, like a kitten at a ball of string. She
missed something: her body told her so, insisted, forced her to
try to remedy it and fill the vacuum. But now her body is old; it
no longer remembers that it missed anything, and all she has left

---

[14]See Joseph Blotner, *Faulkner: A Biography* (New York: Random House, 1974), II,
1440–41.

is a habit, the ghost of a need to rectify something the lack of which her body has long since forgotten about." Fairchild remonstrates with himself for having failed to understand his hostess's motive. "Missed it clean," he thinks. But a few minutes later, standing before Gordon's statue of the naked torso, Fairchild misses it again. He sees in the abstraction a nymph "on a May morning, bathing in a pool where there were a lot of poplar trees." And he exclaims, comparing the statue with the mask of Mrs. Maurier he has just been looking at, "Now, this is the way to forget your grief." Gordon, who has remained silent, cries out a sentiment that Faulkner was to repeat several times: "Forget grief. . . . Only an idiot has no grief; only a fool would forget it. What else is there in this world sharp enough to stick to your guts?" [15]

The movement in *Mosquitoes* out of Gordon's sublimation in art of his personal erotic suffering toward a more comprehensive grasp of the suffering of the human heart is consummated in the nighttown scene which follows the conversation in Gordon's studio. Taken out of context the scene in which the Semitic man, Fairchild, and Gordon, all drunk, wander about the French Quarter represents probably the silliest writing Faulkner ever allowed to get into print; but in the framework of the novel, which however flawed is deliberate, it serves its purpose: to provide an ironic contrast between a redemptive vision of art, history, and sexuality fused in the image of a "Passion Week of the heart"—a transcendent "instant of timeless beatitude"—and the modern sexual incapacity. [16] The nighttown scene is immediately preceded by the account of the visit the dilettantish poet Mark Frost makes to the quarters of Miss Jameson, whose efforts to seduce Mark are singularly nonproductive. The nighttown scene is immediately followed by a further episode (and this

---

[15]*Mosquitoes*, 326–29.
[16]*Ibid.*, 339. See pp. 335–40 for the nighttown scene.

episode concludes the novel) in the blundering sexual career of Mr. Talliaferro. Tricked into Mrs. Maurier's cabin during the journey aboard the *Nausikka,* he is to marry her. But he is still trying to make a conquest of Jenny, one of the desirable young creatures on the voyage. In the total context of *Mosquitoes* you might say that a kind of world historical failure of sexuality emerges as its dominant theme.

It is important to note that the setting of *Mosquitoes* is not simply that of an exotic but anonymous city. It is no doubt far more appropriate for Pan to return to the Vieux Carré than to the courthouse square in a Georgia village; and Faulkner makes the most of the exoticism of a place which broods "in a faintly tarnished languour like an aging yet still beautiful courtesan in a smokefilled room, avid yet weary too of ardent ways." [17] But for all that he makes of its exotic qualities, New Orleans is a historical actuality in *Mosquitoes.* Faulkner knew it as the great port city of the Mississippi valley culture, integral in the history of Mississippi—even though to a north Mississippian like himself, Memphis was the basic metropolitan reference. Faulkner, moreover, knew the French Quarter in the 1920s as the historical setting of a literary and artistic life of some consequence. His involvement in this life was brief, but it was enough for one who assimilated experiences as rapidly and fully as the precocious young writer did. While *Mosquitoes* can be dismissed as an inconsequential, talky novel about arty people (Faulkner himself once referred to it as "trashily smart"),[18] I feel it represents the most substantial experience of modern cultural history Faukner had had up to the point when he wrote the book. In it the young literary artist not only confirmed his initial perception of sexuality as a fundamental motive in the continuum of the historical consciousness but reinforced his feeling that this continuum

---

[17]*Ibid.,* 10.
[18]Faulkner to Horace Liveright, February, 1928, in Blotner (ed.), *Selected Letters of Faulkner,* 40.

cannot be transcended. The tensional relation between Gordon's marble statue of the young girl and the clay mask of Mrs. Maurier symbolizes the way in which even the perfected work of art is in and of history. However awkwardly, *Mosquitoes* presents a myth of the artist as creature of history. Writing this novel, after first living it as a resident of the French Quarter, Faulkner became a self-conscious participant in what many years later he would refer to as the "literary history of man's spirit." [19]

At about the time he completed *Mosquitoes*, Faulkner conceived a more subtle and intricate return of the classical deities into history: this time into northern Mississippi, the country of his nativity, and as it proved to be (after his sojourn in New Orleans and a tour of Europe), the site of his permanent residence. He began work on two stories, one set in Jefferson, the seat of Yoknapatawpha County, the other in Frenchman's Bend, a settlement about ten miles away. The latter story, called *Father Abraham*, introduced a character named Flem Snopes, president of the bank in Jefferson. Several years earlier this son of the tenant farming class had "appeared unheralded" in Jefferson "behind the counter of a small restaurant on a side street, patronized by country people. With this foothold and like Abraham of old, he led his family piece by piece into town." [20] In the course of his rise the impotent Flem marries Eula Varner, pregnant daughter of Will Varner, owner of the general store in Frenchman's Bend and lord of the region. Supplying Eula's need for a husband, Flem gains a hold on Varner. A "softly ample girl with eyes like cloudy hothouse grapes and a mouth always slightly open," [21] Eula is more than a nymph; she is potentially an earth goddess. And so she becomes fifteen years later in *The Hamlet*, the first volume in the Snopes trilogy.

---

[19] Frederick L. Gwynn and Joseph Blotner (eds.), *Faulkner in the University* (New York: Vintage Books, 1965), 130.
[20] *Flags in the Dust*, ed. Douglas Day (New York: Random House, 1973), 154.
[21] Blotner, *Faulkner*, I, 528.

In the resumption of the Snopes story (which Faulkner soon suspended in the 1920s in favor of *Flags in the Dust*), Flem also assumes something of a supratemporal aspect. This is obliquely suggested in the tall tale Ratliff imagines or dreams about the money-obsessed Flem usurping the throne of the Prince of Darkness. In *The Hamlet* Flem is not only a kind of demonic presence but, in the context of Faulkner's subtle parody of pastoral, he may be an instance of Pan transformed into the devil. The possibility of such a transformation is to be found in the Gothic lore and legend of Pan. At about the time Faulkner was writing the *Father Abraham* fragment, the Gothic Pan was being employed directly by Eugene O'Neill in one of his major dramas, *The Great God Brown* (first produced in 1925). In this play, one surely familiar to Faulkner (who admired O'Neill and was, as Blotner shows, influenced by him earlier), the elaborate employment of Greek dramatic masks includes Dion Anthony's exchange of the mask of Pan for that of Mephistopheles. As it is put in the play, "When Pan was forbidden the light and warmth of the sun he grew sensitive and self-conscious and proud and revengeful—and became Prince of Darkness." [22] Further evidence that Faulkner had Flem and Eula in mind as avatars of pastoral deities when he began *Father Abraham* appears in a "highly emblematic" sketch on the back of one page of the manuscript. This depicts Faulkner himself as a faun, or it may be as Pan, piping music to dancing lambs. [23]

By the time he wrote *The Hamlet*, Faulkner knew how the intracosmic beings become creatures of the historical consciousness, and he understood their continuity in the human consciousness of sexuality. He knew that in their return they represent an ironic nexus of the cosmological and historical modes of consciousness. But such comprehension came after

[22]*Ibid.*, 331–32; Merivale, *Pan the Goat-God*, 220.
[23]Blotner, *Faulkner*, I, 529–31.

Faulkner had explored the representation of the nexus through characters more intimately accessible to his imagination than the "peasants" of Frenchman's Bend, namely the Sartorises and the Compsons. Upon discovering the greater accessibility of characters closer to his own class and education, it can be plausibly conjectured, Faulkner temporarily abandoned the "peasants" for the "aristocrats." Thus he found his way directly into the drama of the modern juncture of cosmic and historical. An excited letter he wrote to his publisher Horace Liveright as he finished *Flags in the Dust* seems to confirm this observation: "I have written THE book, of which those other things [*Soldiers' Pay* and *Mosquitoes*] were but foals. I believe it is the damdest best book you'll look at this year, and any other publisher." [24] Having created the foals, Faulkner had now created the mare. Growing in his perception of the ironic complexities involved in the novelist's experience of modern history, he had for the first time in the story of the Sartorises and the Jefferson community fully perceived at its center a crisis in sexuality; and not only this but had found in the history of the South a singular yet compelling representative exemplification of this crisis. He had discovered in the post–Civil War southern consciousness, as embodied in Yoknapatawpha County, an emblem of the modern experience of psychic—of spiritual—estrangement from a unified human existence.

In *Flags in the Dust* the crisis in the historical consciousness of sexuality is located in the character of the matriarchal society that arose in the South after the defeat of the southern men. It was the men, Faulkner once explained, "that couldn't bear being—having lost the war. The women were the ones that could bear it because they never had surrendered. The men had given up and in a sense were dead and even generations later

---

[24]*Ibid.*, 557.

were seeking death." [25] (Of course the time scheme here is exaggerated; the post–Civil War generations may be reckoned realistically as confined to two, or no more than three. Yet those who know the South may well feel that the search for death is not an extinct motive in white southern males, even in the fourth and fifth generations.)

The most interesting character in *Flags in the Dust*, surely the chief character, is Narcissa. A feminine avatar of the mythological youth Narcissus, while her brother Horace is the male avatar, Narcissa falls prey by her own volition to an avatar of the satanic Pan, the obscene letter writer, Byron Snopes. She is a corruption of the matriarchal order (represented in its purity by Aunt Jenny Dupre, Colonel Sartoris's widowed sister) and its struggle to preserve the sacramental family in the face of an abdicated masculinity. She may be a greater corrupter of the family order than the scheming Belle Mitchell, who lures the idealistic Horace from his submissive and basically incestuous relation with his sister into the trap of a long and unhappy marriage. Narcissa is enigmatic in her ways. Having married the death-seeking Bayard Sartoris, borne Bayard's son and on the same day learned of her husband's death in an air crash, she names the son Benbow, instead of giving him his grandfather's name, John, as was expected. Her motive would seem to lie in the hope of removing her son from the Sartoris destiny, but the act may be prompted by a motive that will damn the son more than the Sartoris blood: her desire to enclose him in her own incestuous nature.

All of Narcissa's instincts had been antipathetic to him [Bayard]; his idea was a threat and his presence a violation of the very depths of her nature: in the headlong violence of him she had been like a lily in a gale which rocked to its roots in a sort of vacuum, without any actual laying-on of hands. And now the gale had gone on; the lily had forgotten it as its fury died away into fading vibrations of old terrors and dreads, and the stalk recovered and the bell itself was untarnished save

[25]Gwynn and Blotner (eds.), *Faulkner in the University*, 254.

by the friction of its own petals. The gale is gone, and though the lily is sad a little with vibrations of ancient fears, it is not sorry.[26]

Narcissa's inviolable narcissism may be taken as a singular phenomenon, but in its context in *Flags in the Dust* it suggests the final stage of a South living its death in history, a closure of the southern matriarchy in itself. In this suggestion Faulkner at last clearly sounds a theme he had been seeking to articulate: the internalization of sexuality in the individual of the modern historical society. Faulkner was on the verge of perceiving that the modern sexual situation—as exemplified in the fragmentation of the sacramental family in the twentieth-century South—not only signifies an isolation of the individual in history but an isolation of history in the individual, a closure of history in the self. When at the end of *Flags in the Dust* Faulkner envisioned Narcissa—her child asleep in its crib upstairs in Narcissa's room—quietly playing the piano in the Mississippi twilight, "her white dress with its black ribbon at the waist vaguely luminous in the gloom," and the smell of jasmine drifting in through the window and Miss Jenny listening,[27] he made his final preparation for a very different, far more complex, but congruent vision: that of a fourteen-year-old girl in a flowering pear tree. She has on a "prissy dress" and wears a hat with flowers on it, but her most obvious article of apparel to the children, white and black, who watch from below as she stands precariously in the tree outside a room in the Compson house in Jefferson, is her muddy white drawers.

A snake crawled out from under the house, Jason said he wasn't afraid of snakes and Caddy said he was but she wasn't and Versh said they both were and Caddy said to be quiet, like father said. . . .

---

[26]*Flags in the Dust*, 368.
[27]*Ibid.*, 369.

We stopped under the wet tree by the parlor window. Versh set me down in the wet grass. It was cold. There were lights in all the windows.

"That's where Damuddy is." Caddy said. "She's sick every day now. When she gets well we're going to have a picnic."

"I knows what I knows." Frony said.

The trees were buzzing, and the grass.

"The one next to it is where we have the measles." Caddy said. "Where do you and T. P. have the measles, Frony."

"Has them just wherever we is, I reckon." Frony said.

"They haven't started yet." Caddy said.

They are getting ready to start, T.P. said. You stand right here now while I get that box so we can see in the window. Here, les finish drinking this here sassprilluh. It make me feel just like a squinch owl inside.

We drank the sassprilluh and T.P. pushed the bottle through the lattice, under the house, and went away. I could hear them in the parlor and I clawed my hands against the wall. T.P. dragged the box. He fell down, and he began to laugh. He lay there, laughing into the grass. He got up and dragged the box under the window, trying not to laugh.

"I skeered I going to holler." T.P. said. "Git on the box and see is they started."

"They haven't started because the band hasn't come yet." Caddy said.

"I knows what I knows." Frony said.

"You dont know anything." Caddy said. She went to the tree. "Push me up, Versh."

"Your paw told you to stay out that tree." Versh said.

"That was a long time ago." Caddy said. "I expect he's forgotten about it. Besides, he said to mind me tonight. Didn't he say to mind me tonight."

"I'm not going to mind you." Jason said. "Frony and T.P. are not going to either."

"Push me up, Versh." Caddy said.

"All right." Versh said. "You the one going to get whipped. I aint." He went and pushed Caddy up into the tree to the first limb. We watched the muddy bottom of her drawers. Then we couldn't see her. We could see the tree thrashing.

"Mr. Jason said if you break that tree he whip you." Versh said.

"I'm going to tell on her too." Jason said.
The tree quit thrashing. We looked into the still branches.
"What you seeing." Frony whispered.
I saw them. Then I saw Caddy, with flowers in her hair, and a long veil like shining wind. Caddy. Caddy. . . .
"Who in that tree." Dilsey said. She came and looked up into the tree. "Caddy." Dilsey said. The branches began to shake again.
"You, Satan." Dilsey said. "Come down from there."
"Hush." Caddy said, "Dont you know Father said to be quiet." Her legs came in sight and Dilsey reached up and lifted her out of the tree.[28]

This sequence comes, as you know, from the pear tree episode in the Benjy section of *The Sound and the Fury*. Transpiring in the decayed garden of the Compson place with its "weedchoked traces of the old ruined lawns and promenades," [29] this episode is a memory of the story of the Edenic fall. This was a fall not into simple human mortality but into the linear sexuality of familial generations. It marks the beginning of history in the "generations of Adam." Following the emphasis in Faulkner's poem "Beneath the apple tree Eve's tortured shape," the story of Caddy in the pear tree envisions the subjection both of man and the old non-Edenic gods to the god of human history, the Hebraic Satan. As she comes to us in Benjy's re-creation, Caddy is an avatar of all the women who have borne heirs to the Compson lineage, a Compson princess, a sacred vessel of the family's perpetuation and a symbol of living motherhood. She is also an avatar of Persephone, the goddess of fertility and queen of Hades.[30] She is also an avatar of the Grecian nymphs of the woods and waters. She is also herself, a daring little girl, who is braver than her brothers and who is almost a woman.

---

[28]*The Sound and the Fury* (New York: Vintage Books, 1946), 45–54.
[29]*Ibid.* (Appendix), 409.
[30]Cf. André Bleikasten, *The Most Splendid Failure: Faulkner's The Sound and the Fury* (Bloomington: Indiana University Press, 1976), 43–66. Bleikasten sees the treatment of Caddy as "the quest for Eurydice." The association is possible, but it seems unlikely that it was in Faulkner's mind.

At this point in *The Sound and the Fury* she is none of these things save in a consciousness in which time does not exist; yet which, although responsive to pasture and firelight, is locked in the reverberations of a bodiless name, "Caddy. Caddy" (bodiless because Benjy remembers only the loss not the person) that echoes the historical doom of the Compsons. Like Herman Melville, Thomas Mann, Robinson Jeffers, and Eugene O'Neill, Faulkner was attracted to the relationship between brother and sister as a profound symbol of the modern internalization of history. In the Compson family the symbol is connected with the lapse of the southern matriarchal order as signified by the death of Damuddy, the neurosis of Mrs. Compson, and, most of all, by the fate of Caddy and her daughter, the last Quentin. Faulkner forcefully pursues the symbol of the brother-sister relation into the consciousness of Quentin in the second section of *The Sound and the Fury*, achieving what may well be an unmatched realization of his novelistic powers. In Quentin's story the self (in old-fashioned terminology the "soul") is closed not in the obsessive memorialization of loss, a characteristic of the modern society of science and history, but in a more central, perhaps *the* central imperative of this society: the compulsion, common alike to Francis Bacon and Cotton Mather, to destroy myth and tradition, ritual and liturgy, the wholeness of the sacramental world, in the interest of purifying the consciousness of everything that is not historical. Or, put another way, in the interest of making the individual consciousness absolutely historical.

The compulsive fusion of historical consciousness and self-consciousness, or history and self—this is the meaning of the matchless beginning of the Quentin section: "When the shadow of the sash appeared on the curtains it was between seven and eight o'clock and then I was in time again, hearing the watch. It was Grandfather's and when Father gave it to me he said, Quentin, I give you the mausoleum of all hope and desire."[31] Identifying death, the Crucifixion, and incest with watch and clock, twisting the hands off his watch, recollecting the watch charm from the great world's fair (symbol of the society of science and history), breaking the crystal of his watch and leaving the mark of his blood on the dial—in doing these things Quentin prepares for the consummation of his unwilling, agonizing, but fierce and dedicated compulsion to purify history by drowning himself. Thereby he fulfills what his psychic incest with his sister had signified: the ultimate historical act, a pure identification of his consciousness with the historical death of the Compson family and the South.

In the Jason section of *The Sound and the Fury*, Jason's relation with Caddy becomes a symbol of the closure of history in the self through the purity of Jason's absorption in the money ethic of modern rationalistic society, which, cleansed of myth and tradition and the sacramental connection of life to its sources in nature, makes money the nexus between human beings, even between brother and sister. Told from the authorial point of view, the last section of *The Sound and the Fury* develops the climactic moment in the novel when, in the Easter service in Dilsey's church, the story of Caddy and her brothers is brought into conjunction with the celebration, not of the sacrament of the mass and the transubstantial reality of Christ's presence, but with the historical reality of the events of the Crucifixion and the Resurrection—with Dilsey's endurance of history, its beginning and ending, as sustained by "the annealment and the blood of the remembered Lamb." [32] In his Easter sermon, abandoning his educated manner and becoming the vernacular black preacher, the Reverend Shegog (of Chicago) tells the story of Jesus and the Roman Empire, offering a pure—a puritan, a Pauline—version of the apocalyptic closure of history in the Christ.

---

[31]*The Sound and the Fury*, 93.
[32]*Ibid.*, 371.

In the final moment of the fourth section of *The Sound and the Fury* the order of Benjy's world is associated with the South's attempt to close history in its dream of a modern, world beneficent slave society, and with the defeat of this dream. Luster drives Benjy—gelded, completely innocent of history, yet the complete historian—around the Confederate monument in the courthouse square of Jefferson. The soldier gazes with empty eyes beneath his marble hand, and Benjy, his eyes empty and serene, sees everything in its ordered place. History is closed in the consciousness of a world historical idiot.

In a remarkable comment on his writing of *The Sound and the Fury*, composed in 1933 but not published until recently, Faulkner says: "The story is all there, in the first section as Benjy told it. I did not try deliberately to make it obscure; when I realised that the story might be printed, I took three more sections, all longer than Benjy's, to try to clarify it." The last section, he says, is an effort "to get completely out of the book." In making this endeavor, Faulkner realized "that there would be compensations, that in a sense I could then give a final turn to the screw and extract some ultimate distillation." [33]

If there is an ultimate distillation of the meaning of *The Sound and the Fury*, it comes in the coda to the novel Faulkner wrote some fifteen years after its completion, the Compson genealogy, notably in the entry on Candace Compson. In reporting on Caddy's life after she has left Jefferson, Faulkner presumably moves as far outside his novel as he could ever have gotten without starting over and rewriting it. His movement outward comprehends a further attempt to clarify the Benjy section. After recording Caddy's marital career up to the time of the Nazi invasion of France, where she is living at the time, Faulkner reports that she has vanished in the occupation. But there is a definite clue as to her whereabouts as late as 1943, when Melissa

---

[33]"An Introduction to *The Sound and the Fury*," in Meriwether (ed.), *A Faulkner Miscellany*, 160–61.

Meek, the town librarian of Jefferson, finds a picture in a slick magazine. It is "a picture filled with luxury and money and sunlight—a Cannebière backdrop of mountains and palms and cypresses and the sea, an open powerful expensive chromium-trimmed sports car, the woman's face hatless between a rich scarf and a seal coat, ageless and beautiful, cold serene and damned; beside her a handsome lean man of middle-age in the ribbons and tabs of a German staffgeneral." Melissa clips the picture, puts it in her purse, and goes to Jason. Unfolding it before him she whispers, "It's Caddy . . . . We must save her!" Jason says, "It's Cad, all right"; but then he denies his sister, "That Candace? . . . That bitch aint thirty yet. The other one's fifty now." Desperate, Melissa gets on a train and goes up to Memphis, where Dilsey now lives in the care of Frony. But Dilsey says she is too blind to look at the picture. Melissa comes back to Jefferson, "crying quietly *that was it she didn't want to see it know whether it was Caddy or not because she knows Caddy doesn't want to be saved hasn't anything anymore worth being saved for nothing worth being lost that she can lose.*" [34]

The story of the Compson family ends in Caddy's identification with the unspeakable Nazi endeavor to effect a final purification of history. Serene in her prolonged beauty, Caddy knows her damnation. One more turn of the screw. Dilsey not only knows that Caddy has nothing to be saved for, she knows that Caddy could never have been saved. She recognized this long ago when she said to the little girl in the blooming pear tree. "You, Satan . . . Come down from there." And Caddy said, "Hush. . . . Don't you know Father said to be quiet." Finally recognizing what Dilsey had said, Faulkner got out of *The Sound and the Fury* by turning the story over to the snake in the Compson garden. The only one of the Compsons capable of loving another person (save the servant Dilsey), Caddy emerges

---

[34]*The Sound and the Fury* (Appendix), 415–20.

in her last appearance in the Compson record as an avatar of Satan. Far from being an Arcadian nymph, far even from being Persephone, goddess of the classical underworld, she is an empress of the dark dominion of modern history—the queen of the twentieth-century version of the Hebraic-Christian hell.

In all this oblique emblematizing there is a bizarre but logical extension of what Faulkner refers to in the 1933 introduction to *The Sound and the Fury* as the "symbology of the soiled drawers"—of the "muddy bottom of a little doomed girl climbing a blooming pear tree in April to look in the window at the funeral." [35] The sexuality of the Compsons has become symbolic not simply of the history of the South but, identified with the Nazi imperatives, of the modern drive to control history through the power of the human will. Closed in Caddy, the tale of the Compsons becomes a pure distillation of the terrible intimacy between the individual and modern history. As in her brother Quentin's case, Caddy is not only isolated in history but history is isolated in her.

His preception of the situation of Quentin and Caddy dramatizes the fundamental insight Faulkner attained in writing *The Sound and the Fury*: the knowledge of his own internalization of history, of the closure of history in himself. Exploring the sexuality of southern history, Faulkner underwent a deep experience of the historicism of his own consciousness. This experience is more or less overtly recorded in the 1933 commentary on the composition of *The Sound and the Fury*. (By the time this commentary was written, the experience of history it sets forth had been confirmed in the writing of *As I Lay Dying, Light in August,* and *Sanctuary,* and it was going to be still more deeply confirmed in the writing of *Absalom, Absalom!*) "Because it is himself that he is writing about, not about his environment," the author says in the 1933 document, "he has, figuratively speak-

---

[35] "Introduction to *The Sound and the Fury*," 159, 161.

ing, taken the artist in him in one hand and his milieu in the other and thrust the one into the other like a clawing and spitting cat into a croker sack." [36]

Like Joyce, Faulkner responded directly to the interiority of history first detected by Shakespeare and Cervantes. This followed upon the loss of the cosmic sacramentalism which the medieval society of myth and tradition had perpetuated, but which could not survive the attack on it by the sixteenth- and seventeeth-century reformers bent on redeeming Christianity by reclaiming the apocalyptic historicism of St. Paul. Like Joyce, Faulkner was attracted to the notion that the apocalypse of history in the self of the artist dispenses with God and elevates the artist to the throne. Indeed, Faulkner in one well-known statement (1959) ironically assumes the whole foundation of Yoknapatawpha to rest on his godlike power paradoxically to create a sacramental cosmos out of his particular experience of the historicism of consciousness:

With *Soldiers' Pay* I found out writing was fun. But I found out afterward that not only each book had to have a design but the whole output or sum of an artist's work had to have a design. With *Soldiers' Pay* and *Mosquitoes* I wrote for the sake of writing because it was fun. Beginning with *Sartoris* I discovered that my own little postage stamp of native soil was worth writing about and I would never live long enough to exhaust it, and that by sublimating the actual into the apocryphal I would have complete liberty to use whatever talent I might have to its absolute top. It opened up a gold mine of other people, so I created a cosmos of my own. I can move these poeple around like God, not only in space but in time too. The fact that I have moved my characters around in time successfully, at least in my estimation, proves to me my own theory that time is a fluid condition which has no existence except in the momentary avatars of individual people. There is no such thing as *was*—only *is*. If *was* existed, there would be no grief or sorrow. I like to think of the world I created as

---

[36]*Ibid.*, 158.

being a kind of keystone in the universe; that, small as that keystone is, if it were ever taken away the universe itself would collapse. My last book will be the Doomsday Book, the Golden Book, of Yoknapatawpha County. Then I shall break the pencil and I'll have to stop.[37]

Saying that beginning with *Sartoris* ("the germ of my apocrypha")[38] he sublimated the actual—that is to say the basic sexuality of southern history he discovered in the initial Yoknapatawpha novel, or more precisely, the matriarchal culture of Mississippi—into the apocryphal, is not Faulkner wryly saying more than that he translated social reality into fiction or, for that matter, that he elevated it into myth? Does he not imply something like the transformation of the actual into a secular testament—into pseudo, or, it may be, uncanonized scripture? In the sense either of that which is testamentary or of that which has "hidden meanings" (the more literal sense of the term), "apocryphal" may appropriately characterize stories which in total design constitute a massive replication of the conjunction of the cosmic and historical modes of existence—and not less the result of this conjunction in the literary imagination, the recognition of the absorption of the cosmic in the historical. Yoknapatawpha, Faulkner's apocryphal world, is a great, ironic, often enigmatic testament to the capacity of the literary imagination to conceive the drama of the historical consciousness in its formation and in its completion and to conceive this as a tale told by the modern literary artist. To return to the metaphor with which I began, Yoknapatawpha is a part of the large edifice of Western secular literature. Since the age of Marlowe and Shakespeare and Cervantes and before, since the time when Christendom began to purify itself of the medieval cosmic sacramentalism (and since the time when the purifiers came to

---

[37]Jean Stein Vanden Heuvel, "William Faulkner" [interview], in *Writers at Work: The Paris Review Interviews*, ed. Malcolm Cowley (New York: Viking Press, 1959), 141.
[38]Gwynn and Blotner (eds.), *Faulkner in the University*, 285.

America to establish New England and eventually the South, which today is the American homeland of the "born again") this construct has always been enlarging and more and more assuming the status of secular scripture. Not opposite to but apposite to the religious structure erected on the Protestant vision of the Bible, it is itself, like this vision, a source and integral part of the Western imagination of history.

Faulkner the Innovator

ALBERT J. GUERARD

I will begin with the dogmatic assertion that Faulkner was, all things considered, the greatest innovator in the history of American fiction. "All things considered" means that due attention has been given to both Melville and Gertrude Stein, and means acknowledging that Joyce was not American. Faulkner was the greatest innovator because he both freed language from the spare austerity of Hemingway and his imitators, and freed structure from the rectilinear and mimetic controls of the great nineteenth- and twentieth-century realists. The curve of Faulkner's career shows a growing dissatisfaction with the inherited novel form, an ultimate recognition that a "novel" could be anything: could even interlace, in *Requiem for a Nun*, dithyrambic historical essay and poetic drama. Faulkner judged his contemporaries by the risks they took. But none took risks comparable to those of *Absalom, Absalom!* or even *The Sound and the Fury*.

These assertions could be defended even if it were true (and it isn't) that Faulkner's eccentricities were those of a writer incapable of traditional mastery. They would be true even if we accepted Faulkner's version of why he wrote *The Sound and the Fury* as he did. And they would be true even if we saw, behind Faulkner's counterpointed plots, the double plots of Shake-speare and Dickens, or behind the strange mixture of modes and tonalities, the blendings of reality and fantasy, say *The Tempest* and *Midsummer Night's Dream*. The young novelist looking about him in the mid and late 1920s would normally be most conscious of Hemingway and Fitzgerald and, of course, Sherwood Anderson. What Faulkner did—like Djuna Barnes in *Nightwood*, like John Hawkes later in *The Cannibal*—was to break totally with the accepted fictional norms.

All this seems obvious. Yet it is astonishing how little attention has been given to these innovations and to Faulkner's aesthetic *playfulness* generally. The moralist and psychologist, the historian and sociologist of the South, the compassionate and extravagant story-teller . . . these have had infinitely more attention than the artist.

For the moment I shall merely block out several kinds of Faulknerian innovation.[1]

Streams of Consciousness, and the Significance of Italics
As I Lay Dying—however rapidly written by a power plant employee on an overturned wheelbarrow—was an extremely original book, a French *nouveau roman* twenty-six years before Robbe Grillet's *Le Voyeur*. "One real originality" was "its juxtaposition, startling for 1929, of the tragic or pathetic and the farcical. But its great technical problem was to render communal, ritual, largely physical movement through counterpointed solitary consciousnesses. This compounded the initial difficulty of conveying an ongoing present through very brief interior monologues rather than long or retrospective ones."[2] *As I Lay Dying* strikes me as a *tour de force*, as does the Benjy section of *The Sound and the Fury*: ingenious, impressive, but appealing most of all to critics who enjoy solving puzzles. I will even sacrilegiously venture that I wish the grand macabre ritual pro-

---

[1]Some of these are discussed in Chapter 8, "Faulkner: Problems of Technique" in my *The Triumph of the Novel: Dickens, Dostoevsky, Faulkner* (New York, 1976), 204–34, and at various other places in the book. Narration by conjecture in *Absalom, Absalom!* is discussed on pp. 332–38 of the same volume.
[2]*Ibid.*, 206.

cession of the Bundrens had been written in the richer prose and with the richer incongruities of *The Hamlet*. The final pages of Quentin's section are very beautiful, where a remembered door is also the Door between life and death,

> . . . and that's it if people could only change one another forever that way merge like a flame swirling up for an instant then blowing cleanly out along the cool eternal dark instead of lying there trying not to think of the swing until all cedars came to have that vivid dead smell of perfume that Benjy hated so. Just by imagining the clump it seemed to me that I could hear whispers secret surges smell the beating of hot blood under wild unsecret flesh watching aginst red eyelids the swine untethered in pairs rushing coupled into the sea and he we must just stay awake and see evil done for a little while.[3]

But even these lines hardly belong with the best lines of *Ulysses*.

Faulkner's striking innovation is rather to explore and convey different levels of consciousness—from full conscious notation to an unconscious mind of Jungian powers of memory and even powers of foreknowledge—and to do this within the space of a few lines. There is, for instance, the young Joe Christmas's confusion as he watches Bobbie Allen behind the counter, and the men with their slanted hats who speak to her through the cigarette smoke. We go beneath the level of normal consciousness when, perversely, Faulkner says "thinking" and then moves from roman to italics, conveying at least four levels of consciousness.

> *"I don't even know what they are saying to her,"* he thought, thinking *I don't even know that what they are saying to her is something that men do not say to a passing child* believing *I do not know yet that in the instant of sleep the eyelid closing prisons within the eye's self her face demure, pensive; tragic, sad, and young; waiting, colored with all the vague and formless magic of young desire. That already there is something for love to feed upon: that sleeping I know now why I struck*

---

[3]*The Sound and the Fury* (Random House, 1956), 219.

*refraining that negro girl three years ago and that she must know it too
and be proud too, with waiting and pride*
    So he did not expect to see her again, since love in the young
requires as little of hope as of desire to feed upon.[4]

I do not find this experiment entirely convincing. But it opens
the way to very great writing in *Absalom, Absalom!* and "The
Bear." It recognizes that there can be true "knowledge" in the
unconscious mind, that there are divers levels of preconscious-
ness, and, more importantly, that the writer is free to use, must
use, language that the character himself would not know.
    I would like to see a full statistical study of italics in Faulkner,
quite apart from their special signalling usage in the Benjy
section of *The Sound and the Fury.* In *Absalom, Absalom!*,
generally speaking, italics would seem to signify mental
processes that are not normal conscious mental processes and
also to signify speech that is not real speech spoken aloud and
mimetically recorded. The word "thinking" following upon
Quentin's thought that Shreve "sounds just like father" leads to
an italicized deepening or generalizing that partakes of divine
(e.g., Faulknerian) omniscience and humor:

    . . . thinking *Mad impotent old man who realized at last that there must
    be some limit even to the capabilities of a demon for doing harm, who
    must have seen his situation as that of the show girl, the pony, who real-
    izes that the principal tune she prances comes not from horn and fiddle
    and drum but from a clock and calendar, must have seen himself as the
    old wornout cannon which realizes that it can deliver just one more
    fierce shot and crumble to dust in its own furious blast and recoil.*[5]

I have already argued, though I certainly cannot prove, that
Miss Rosa's "notlanguage" was not spoken aloud;[6] that even the

---

[4]*Light in August*, 165–66.
[5]*Absalom, Absalom!*, 181.
[6]*The Triumph of the Novel*, 323.

best southern poetess would not really say to a young man of college age: *"that fond dear constant violation of privacy, that stultification of the burgeoning and incorrigible I which is the meed and due of all mammalian meat, became not mistress, not beloved, but more than even love; I became all polymath love's androgynous advocate."* [7] I think we have a modulation, at the beginning of the fifth chapter, from real speech (*So they will have told you doubtless already how I told that Jones to take that mule*) to a language conveying, in Mr. Compson's distinction, not what was in Miss Rosa's mind but in her soul: what the whole personality (conscious, preconscious, unconscious) would say if it could speak.

As italics may indicate different levels of consciousness, or that dialogue was not really, literally spoken, so too they may crucially suggest a shift in degree of authorial knowledge. In the wonderfully unstable world of *Absalom, Absalom!*, where conjecture so enormously outweighs fact, there comes the time when Quentin and Shreve, identifying with Henry and Charles, the two become four then two again, are actually carried back—the novel, rather, is carried back—to what I think is historical fact. They suddenly, with the italics on page 346, partake of real omniscience. They, and we, are there: "(*—the winter of '64 now, the army retreated across Alabama, into Georgia; now Carolina was just at their backs and Bon, the officer, thinking . . . .*)" The confrontations on the pages to follow, and the crucial dialogues of 351–58, are true, not conjectural history. The italics are not, as Cleanth Brooks argues, the mark of joint visualization. [8]

The novel's final italics, on the other hand, the suppositious exchange between Quentin and Henry Sutpen ("the wasted hands crossed on the breast as if he were already a corpse") seem

---

[7]*Absalom, Absalom!*, 146.
[8]See *The Triumph of the Novel*, 334–35. See also Cleanth Brooks, "The Narrative Structure of *Absalom, Absalom!*," *The Georgia Review* (Summer, 1975), 387.

more problematic. Whatever exchange did occur—spoken or silently intuitive—is the novel's ultimate epistemological foundation. Brooks has timed the exchange, making due allowance for reasonable pauses. But the italicized exchange is meant to suggest, I think, a confrontation and revelation so startling that it could not be rendered mimetically. Instead we have a cinema of Quentin's mind circling in astonishment. We are given less what he heard than what he felt:

> *And you are—?*
> *Henry Sutpen.*
> *And you have been here—?*
> *Four years.*
> *And you came home—?*
> *To die. Yes.*
> *To die?*
> *Yes. To die.*
> *And you have been here—?*
> *Four years.*
> *And you are—?*
> *Henry Sutpen.* [9]

Italics, to sum up, suggest the author is in some way transforming reality and distancing the reader from it. He is forewarning us that mimesis has truly been abandoned, and reminding us a little more forcibly than usual that he can do whatever he pleases with this world he has made: William Faulkner, sole proprietor. Which is not at all to say that this transformed world isn't "true." Thus (in *Requiem*) the "outlander with a B.A. or (perhaps even) M.A. from Harvard or Northwestern or Stanford, passing through Jefferson by chance or accident" and coming upon the legend of Cecilia Farmer—may discover not what "*might* have been, nor even *could* have been, but *was*: so vast, so limitless in capacity is man's imagination to disperse and burn away the rubble-dross of fact and probability, leaving only truth and dream."

---

[9]*Absalom, Absalom!*, 373.

Narration by Conjecture

I have talked at some length, in *The Triumph of the Novel*, about Faulkner's elaborate use of this Conradian technique, adumbrated in *Lord Jim* and more fully exploited in certain chapters of *Chance*. In *Absalom, Absalom!* Faulkner carried to its fullest development a method that, not surprisingly, tempted the very intellectual Thomas Mann in *Joseph and His Brothers*, and that even Hawthorne momentarily employed in *The Blithedale Romance*. It goes without saying that good fiction (and detective fiction of course) has always dramatized puzzled, struggling, conjecturing minds. The difference, at moments in *Chance*, is for conjecture to seem like dramatized fact, and for it even to be, in *Absalom, Absalom!*, dramatized fact:

> Narration by conjecture (in Conrad, and much more in Faulkner) brings the act of conjecturing to the forefront, and makes the struggling speculative mind (as Marlow's or Quentin's) a major interest. Conjecture, after all, is among the most humane of our mental activities— more humane than blind belief, or than flawless reasoning on unassailable evidence. We care not only about what Marlow will discover, but also about the way his subtle mind suavely moves and about his initially reluctant, at last intense involvement in the mysteries he explores. But the major difference from Jamesian studies in ambiguity, the great technical step forward, is to dramatize the events conjectured as though they were true; the accents of speculation shift to those of direct narration or observation. *Conjecture thus becomes a point-of-view and basic vehicle for real story-telling and for the plausible creation of time, place, atmosphere, emotions, events . . . .* A further audacity is the implicit claim that the suppositious acts dramatized as true often *are* true in some higher or metaphysical sense. "History" (say the irrecoverable history of Mississippi 1833–1909, or of Sutpen's arrival in Jefferson) is what, after truly scrupulous effort, we discern it to be. Myth and legend, which inhabit individual and collective consciousness (and the unconscious too), are also components of "history" . . . .
>
> . . . The basic method, then, is to summon up events, scenes, persons through conjecture, then vivify them (with the most efficient verisimilar techniques) as true: *make the reader see.*[10]

[10]*The Triumph of the Novel*, 332–33.

Faulkner the Innovator

Everyone is familiar with the great moments of conjectural narration in *Absalom, Absalom!*—scenes as vivid as any in Dickens or Balzac: the sybaritic corrupting Charles Bon exposing Henry's innocence to the lovely decadence of New Orleans; the events leading to the murder of Sutpen; the murder and its aftermath; the deaths of Milly and Wash Jones; and the puzzled colloquy of Sutpen and Wash, as they stare at each other in an after-life where they "would even have a scuppernong vine for them there and no compulsions now of bread or ambition or fornication or vengeance." The clues to conjectural narration in Faulkner's later novels—*perhaps, maybe, I imagine,* and so on—regularly prepare us for intense and often humorous writing. The discovery of a genially sardonic character who likes to embroider on hearsay—V. K. Suratt, later Ratliff—was a very important one. Small wonder Faulkner had a special fondness for him.

It is interesting once again to look at beginnings. Thus very late in Faulkner's second novel, *Mosquitoes,* we have the Semitic man's story of Mrs. Maurier's marriage. The novel has, in its earlier pages, a number of pleasing audacities. But not a few of them seem borrowed audacities, with the author in the unnatural role of weary presiding sophisticate. For one thing he is clearly not comfortable with the need to report so much dialogue directly and so much present scene; congenial distance is lacking. But the story of Mrs. Maurier's marriage takes us back to some very vivid writing in Conrad's *Chance.* There Marlow's screening meditative comment intensifies the conjectured scene, and the conjectured anguish of a baffled scheming governess:

"And all this torture for nothing, in the end! What looked at last like a possible prize (oh, without illusions! but still a prize) broken in her hands, fallen in the dust, the bitter dust, of disappointment, she revelled in the miserable revenge—pretty safe too—only regretting the unworthiness of the girlish figure which stood for so much she had longed to be able to spit venom at, if only once, in perfect liberty. The presence of the young man at her back increased both her satisfaction and her rage. But the very violence of the attack seemed to defeat its end by rendering the representative victim as it were insensible." [11]

The young Faulkner of *Mosquitoes* is not quite ready to write at this level of controlled intensity. But there are moments in the thousand-word narrative of Mrs. Maurier's marriage that promise the irony and compassion of the major novels. I will read a few sentences here and there, moments in which the technique—narration by conjecture—engages the true Faulknerian play of mind:

"The story is that her father came to New Orleans on a business trip, with a blessing from Washington. She was young, then; probably a background of an exclusive school, and a social future, the taken-for-granted capital letter kind, but all somehow rather precarious— cabbage, and a footman to serve it; a salon in which they sat politely, surrounded by objects, and spoke good French; and bailiff's men on the veranda and the butcher's bill in the kitchen—gentility: evening clothes without fresh linen underneath. I imagine he—her father—was pretty near at the end of his rope. Some government appointment, I imagine, brought him south: highjacking privileges with official sanction, you know.

"The whole family seemed to have found our climate salubrious, though, what with hibiscus and mimosa on the lawn instead of bailiffs, and our dulcet airs after the rigors of New England; and she cut quite a figure among the jeunesse dorée of the nineties; fell in love with a young chap, penniless but real people, who led cotillions and went without gloves to send her flowers and glacé trifles from the rue Vendôme and sang to a guitar among the hibiscus and mimosa when stars were wont to rise." [12]

And the wedding, scarcely more auspicious than Thomas Sutpen's and Ellen's:

"I'd like to have seen her, coming out of the church afterward. They would have had a canopy leading from the door to the carriage: there

---

[11]*Chance* (Kent ed.), 120.
[12]*Mosquitoes* (Liveright, 1955) 324–25.

must have been a canopy, and flowers, heavy ones—Lochinvar would have sent gardenias; and she, decked out in all the pagan trappings of innocence and her beautiful secret face beside that cold, violent man, graying now, but you have remarked how it takes the harlequinade of aristocracy to really reveal peasant blood, haven't you? And her Lochinvar to wish her godspeed, watching her ankles as she got into the carriage." [13]

This brief evocation of the wedding suggests how, in the best sense, the technique's advantages are double-edged. The speaker, since he was not an eyewitness, can be exceedingly brief and selective. He can permit himself a highly suggestive vagueness. He was not there to observe the dress in detail, and so can say "decked out in all the pagan trappings of innocence." But he can also focus on a vividly intimate conjectured detail: the Lochinvar "watching her ankles as she got into the carriage."

Narration by conjecture, which by definition has no burden of proof, seems particularly suited to the mythically extravagant event, and the event involving, it may be, very complicated physical action. I am thinking of that altogether central event in the history of Frenchman's Bend: the conception of Linda Varner Snopes. You will recall how Eula's five or six baffled suitors ambushed the carriage carrying McCarron and Eula, how Eula drove them off with the buggy whip and how her Olympian virginity was at last voluntarily lost to a man with a newly broken arm. In *The Hamlet* the technique is that of hearsay, which is of course close to narration by conjecture:

Nobody ever knew exactly what happened. There was a house near the ford, but there were no yells and shouts this time, merely abrasions and cuts and missing teeth on four of the five faces seen by daylight tomorrow. The fifth one, the other of the two who had beaten the Negro, still lay unconscious in the nearby house. Someone found the butt of the buggy whip. It was clotted with dried blood and human hair and later, years later, one of them told that it was the girl who had wielded it, springing from the buggy and with the reversed whip

---

beating three of them back while her companion used the reversed pistol-butt against the wagon-spoke and the brass knuckles of the other two. That was all that was ever known.[14]

The sexual encounter itself reaches us very obliquely indeed: Will Varner's "reading of the female heart in general and his daughter's in particular, had been betrayed at the last by failing to anticipate that she would not only essay to, but up to a certain point actually support, with her own braced arm from underneath, the injured side."

It is one of the glories of Faulkner that he repeats himself, and allows us to enjoy the same incident more than once. Thus in *The Mansion*, fifteen years after *The Hamlet*, we have the sexual encounter vividly conjectured by Ratliff. And now we have both more visual detail than hearsay would permit and the priceless fun of Ratliff's commentary:

So it never even stopped. I mean, the motion, movement. It was one continuous natural rush from the moment five of them busted outen that thicket and grabbed at the horse, on through the cussing and trompling and hard breathing and the final crashing through the bushes and the last rapid and fading footfall, since likely the other four thought Theron was dead; then jest the peaceful quiet and the dark road and the horse standing quiet in the buggy in the middle of it and Theron Quick sleeping peacefully in the weeds. And that's when I believe it happened: not no cessation a-tall, not even no active pausing; not just the maiden bastion capitulate and overrun but them loins themselves seeded, that child, that girl, Linda herself created into life right there in the road with likely Eula having to help hold him up offen the broke arm and the horse standing over them among the stars like one of them mounted big-game trophy heads sticking outen the parlor or the liberry or (I believe they call them now) den wall. In fact maybe that's what it was.[15]

A very moving moment in *The Wild Palms*, finally, will

---

[14]*The Hamlet*, 139.
[15]*The Mansion*, 124.

suggest how complex and delicate narration by conjecture can be. Charlotte here suspects that she will, thanks to the botched abortion, very possibly die. She goes home to talk to her husband and she sees her children for a last time. Her purpose is to persuade Rittenmeyer, in the event she does die, to take no action against her lover and unsuccessful abortionist Wilbourne. Wilbourne himself waits outside, sitting on a bench in Audubon Park. And he imagines, creates by conjecture, the scene inside the house. "He could see them, the two of them, Rittenmeyer in the double-breasted suit (it might be flannel now but it would be dark flannel, obtruding smoothly its unobtrusive cut and cost); the four of them, Charlotte here and the three others yonder, the two children who were unremarkable, the daughters," and so on. He could see them, he could hear them: " *'Go speak to your mother, Charlotte. Take Ann with you.'* " With these italicized lines, and for over five pages, Wilbourne's conjecture appears to be omniscient. We seem to have direct reporting of dialogue. But in seven places, returning to roman type, we are also reminded that Wilbourne is waiting outside, and that the reported scene is nominally conjectured. The result is that an intensely emotional confrontation is slightly screened or distanced. In addition we experience to some degree (but at a very considerable distance) Wilbourne's own suffering.

In any event I am sure these distances were necessary to Faulkner's imagination, as it coped with one of the most romantic passages in all his work. Charlotte tells her husband she has one thing to ask of him:

"Of me? A favor?"
"If you like. I dont ask a promise. Maybe what I am trying to express is just a wish. Not hope; wish. If anything happens to me."
"If anything happens to you. What am I to do?"
"Nothing."
"Nothing?"
"Yes. Against him. I dont ask it for his sake nor even for mine. I ask it for the sake of—of—I dont even know what I am trying to say. For the sake of all the men and women who ever lived and blundered

but meant the best and all that ever will live and blunder but mean the best. For your sake maybe, since yours is suffering too–if there is any such thing as suffering, if any of us ever did, if any of us were ever born strong enough and good enough to be worthy to love or suffer either. Maybe what I am trying to say is justice."

"*Justice?*" And now he could hear Rittenmeyer laughing, who had never laughed since laughter is yesterday's slight beard, the negligee among emotions. "*Justice? This, to me? Justice?*" *Now she rises; he too: they face one another.*[16]

It is always embarrassing to turn from Faulkner's beautiful prose to the academic task of summing-up. Narration by conjecture would seem particularly congenial to two writers, Conrad and Faulkner, "who showed remarkable indifference to the literal truth in the accounts of their own lives." [17] I would like to state this even more forcefully. For Conrad, but even more for Faulkner, either imagined experience or remembered real experience was all the more living, all the more true, because it was pricelessly mobile and indeterminate, unfixed in space and time, subject always to imaginative reconstruction. Faulkner's characters, we know, went on growing and changing in his mind; hence his oddly inaccurate recollections of his own books. Or the fact that he could tell me in 1946, as an interesting current event in a distant corner of the county, an anecdote appearing on the third page of *The Hamlet* that, six years before, I had reviewed for the *Boston Evening Transcript*. Narration by conjecture is ideally suited to the writer for whom fact and fiction inextricably interpenetrate, and for whom the world can always be remade.

This beautiful instability of the imagined world is closely related to Conrad's and Faulkner's temperamental evasiveness. It is particularly congenial to the novelist who loves irresolution, and who is reluctant to report experience photographically. For Faulkner as for Conrad the "impressionist method meant freedom from *presentness*, from the obligation to report things

---

[16]*The Wild Palms*, 225–26.
[17]*The Triumph of the Novel*, 336.

happening in a time flowing onward at an even pace, and happening (for the imagination) here and now." And of course the technique, "without sacrificing many of the resources of Flaubertian or other realism (for *anything*, however conjectural, can be intensely visualized), frees the writer from mimesis narrowly conceived, from documentary inhibition, from the need to pretend to be giving an authentic report. The boring obligation to demonstrate authority has been largely removed. For the authority is now that of the speculative mind free to wander in space and time, and always alert to potentiality as well as hard evidence. The method invites the use at every moment of a real speaking voice and (as after all in Sterne) a convincingly wandering mind." [18]

Narration by conjecture is obviously suited to novels concerned with ambiguity, as the very best of Faulkner are. *A Fable*, for all its moments of catastrophic failure, has also its very fine ones. In some of these we see simple, humble people caught up in the mysterious, volitionless movement of history, and dimly aware that the ambiguities around them partake of golden legend. So for instance Marthe/Magda, pleading with the old general for his son's life: "Because we were children, we didn't know: we only watched and saw and knitted, knotted, tried to, what simple threads we had of implication." And I would add what I did not say in *The Triumph of the Novel*, but what I am the more conscious of speaking in this place, in Oxford-Jefferson: narration by conjecture is suited to a land and society so full of legend and myth, and so full of people (most of them not professional writers) who love to tell stories, and who are surely aware of what *Requiem for a Nun* refers to as "the town's composite heritage of remembering."

Which is only to say one more time that a good novel is not a mere document or report on reality, and that a good story-teller incessantly reinvents the world.

---

[18]*Ibid.*, 337.

The "Cracking" of the Novel Form

Nothing is more obvious, as we scan the full curve of Faulkner's career, than the growing dissatisfaction with the inherited form of the standard realistic novel. Very evidently he had the strong impulse, as Durrell said of his own work, to "crack forms" and establish new freedoms. The culminating audacity would appear to be that of *Requiem for a Nun*: the intercalation of poetic play about a much changed Temple Drake and the three superb essays of highly conjectural Mississippi history: "The Courthouse," "The Golden Dome," "The Jail." Not the least audacity was the parody of Shakespeare's famous "This England" soliloquy, here evoking Jackson's golden dome: "this rounded knob, this gilded pustule . . . this knob, this pimple-dome, this buried half-ball hemisphere" in the beginning already decreed. Granted that *Ulysses* remains the great seismic event, in the deconstruction of the novel form, *Requiem for a Nun* would seem altogether as audacious as Nabokov's *Pale Fire*, whose narrative is conveyed through a poem and its scholarly apparatus.

I will merely mention the most obvious instances of cracked form.

The Wild Palms (1939) juxtaposes two narratives occurring at different times: the Tall Convict's heroic rescue in the Mississippi flood of 1927, the doomed lovers fleeing security in the depression year 1938. There are obvious thematic connections: the lovers seeing organized society and its security as destructive to a grand passion; the convict longing to return to the security of the prison farm. But the major aesthetic contrast is between two altogether different modes of narrative—the lovers enacting a story that might have been conceived by Hemingway, with nothing added to what "might really have happened"; the tall convict's story, on the other hand, a grand myth evoking not merely our first parents of Genesis but an apocalyptic vision of flood and dissolution. The two narratives have at times been printed separately, and each can be enjoyed in its own right. But the richest effects come, I think, from the interlocking, from the reader's feelings as he moves back and forth between the grim, spare, dramatic reporting of "Wild Palms" and the highly charged poetry and exaggeration of "Old Man." The question is not merely one of relief, the relief that comes from changed intensities. For to some extent, I suspect, the feeling generated in the reader by one story permeates his reaction to the other.

The logical connections beween the disparate parts of "The Bear" are obvious: Ike's education through the masculine comradeship and the hunting ethic of parts one, two, three, and five; his induction, through the ledgers of part four, into his heritage of evil. The lesson in both is to relinquish, to relinquish the man-made rational aids of gun and watch and compass, in the night journey into self, and to reliquish a tainted material inheritance, since neither people nor property can be owned. But these logical connections are really the delights of the college or even high school classroom. I argued in *The Triumph of the Novel* that the difficulty of part four makes the hunting story, as we return to it in part five, a darker, more meditative experience and, also, that perhaps some interruption of the hunting narrative was necessary before the poignant story of the last hunt. But even this may be rather desperate logic. After numerous readings I find most moving a mysteriousness that pervades the two narratives, and that is reinforced by occult coincidence and strange reflexive reference: the connections made between the bear and that new deity of the woods, the locomotive, and between the locomotive and the archetypal eternal snake; or, even more subtly, by the way the bear, Sam Fathers, and the great blue dog Lion look at Ike meaningfully. For we are in a noumenal world of mysterious intuition and foreknowledge, in which Sam Fathers knows that his own life must be virtually coterminous with the bear's.

The most startling break in a long novel's form is no doubt the intrusion, in *A Fable*, of the "Notes on a Horsethief." There are logical connections again, but more real in the critical quarterly than in a normal humane reading. Here are a few sentences from my own academic formula:

"Notes on a Horsethief" is a story of secular love and its golden legend, juxtaposed against war's "grimed and blood-stained" chronicle (also eternal, though often imaged in terms of ecclesiastical history) and the story of Christ returned to earth to lead a mutiny. In both stories there is a highly emotional drama of public, collective complicity with idealistic individual actions—the theft of the fabulous race-horse (so that he can continue to race, though on three legs, rather than be retired to stud); the Christ-corporal's organizing of the mutiny. In both there is a sense, deeply pessimistic in the war story, of people moving without volition or even awareness of what they are about. All institutions and all hierarchies are doomed to fail; history is a futile spawning of event. But also, consolingly, we see individual human beings struggle in vain against the heroism and idealism thrust upon them.[19]

More important for the nonacademic reader may be the relief that the American interlude provides from the gloom of wartime France. It is good to be back in Mississippi and the South, and to have numerous echoes from earlier novels. (And to be sure there are great pages even in the war narrative. I believe *A Fable* and *Pylon* are the two Faulkners one is warned not to read. But both are very courageous, experimental books. *Pylon* is not, as Camus thought, Faulkner's best. But all Faulkner is worth reading.)

There is much more that could be said about counterpoint and musical form: about the oddity of *Light in August*, for instance, where the central figures of the two stories (Lena and Joe Christmas) never meet, though the Reverend Hightower is traumatically involved with both. The thematic contrast, and the doubling of plots, is perhaps Dickensian—Lena Grove's world of fertility, of naïve trust in life, and unselfconscious acceptance of whatever life brings, whether the seducer Lucas Burch or the

---

[19]*Ibid.*, 208.

savior Byron Bunch; or Joe Christmas's world of fear, hatred, neurotic obsession, compulsion, self-hatred, and self-destruction. And the novel's comic conclusion is an escape, for the reader, from the deep tragedy of Joe Christmas and the gray, pallid story of Hightower's withdrawal.

The grotesque mixture of literary forms, narrative modes, tonalities was not after all a Faulknerian innovation; there had been, for instance, Shakespeare. But the mixture was indeed startling to readers of the late twenties and the thirties—the blend of the farcical and the pathetic or tragic in *Sanctuary* and *As I Lay Dying* and even, briefly, in *Sartoris*. I will take one more public occasion, in concluding, to repudiate my 1940 review of *The Hamlet* for *The Boston Evening Transcript*. To one brought up on the divergent austerities of Ernest Hemingway and Yvor Winters, and for whom Edith Wharton as well as Henry James had been held up as a model, *The Hamlet* did not seem "really a novel." It was, rather, a random collection of brilliant novelettes and stories, a work of disorderly genius. I much prefer my 1976 view of it "as an artful, essentially poetic or musical composition that deliberately mixes modes: naturalism and myth, comedy and pathos, the macabre and the good-humored, violence and natural beauty; the cruel and the sordid distanced and evaluated by language. We may insist on the fact of *compositon*, and on the delicate relationships among the novel's parts, even though we know much rearrangement of earlier writing occurred. For what we have is the published book, and it is, especially after the first two chapters, an exquisitely balanced creation manipulating with assurance a variety of reader responses." [20]

---

[20]*Ibid.*, 213.

Faulkner's Women

ILSE DUSOIR LIND

The anthropologist Margaret Mead once attempted to convey the difference between the older generation and the younger through an imagined conversation between an elder and a youth.[1] In this dialogue the elder says, "I have been young, but you have never been old." The youth replies, "You have never been young in the world in which I am young, and you never can be." The relevance of this proverbial wisdom to the topic "Faulkner's Women" is in its serving as a reminder that for anyone old enough to have observed the growth of Faulkner's reputation over the years, watching successive misapprehensions about his work dissipate, it may seem that there is nothing—or at least very little—that needs to be said on this subject. Faulkner himself said that he found women "fun" to write about, that he found them "marvelous, wonderful."[2] Among those who have been enjoying his work now for half a lifetime, who does not agree that his fiction gives ample evidence of such an attitude?

For those who have already learned how to be comfortable

---

[1]Margaret Mead, *Culture and Commitment, A Study of the Generation Gap* (New York: Doubleday, 1970), 49.
[2]Frederick L. Gwynn and Joseph L. Blotner (eds.), *Faulkner in the University: Class Conferences at the University of Virginia 1957–1958* (Charlottesville, Va., 1959), 45.

with Faulkner's work, in other words, the continuing wonder is only *how* he did it—how he created women characters who hold so permanent a place in memory. Caddy, Dilsey, Addie Bundren, Eula Varner, Linda Snopes—we have only to say their names to make them appear to the mind's eye in all their individuality and color. They live in the reader's imagination the way the women characters of the greatest writers do—as Madame Bovary does, or Lady Macbeth, or Becky Sharpe, or Anna Karénina. For the established reader of Faulkner, then, a discussion of Faulkner's women holds interest only insofar as it promises some new insights into his literary art.

But for those who are now in other phases of their response to Faulkner's fiction, it may be more helpful than otherwise to admit that negative criticism of this aspect of his work has been intense and persistent and that resolution of the problems posed by Faulkner's writing in this area is by no means easy, not even for the most favorably disposed reader. I recall my own experience as a college student when "A Rose for Emily" and *Sanctuary* were assigned. It was the late 1930s; Faulkner's writings dealing with psychopathological women—a subject in which he became especially interested during the early thirties—had only recently begun to appear. I was eighteen, in love with literature, not very worldly. The actions of Emily Grierson and Temple Drake were unthinkable to me, even unimaginable; my extreme distaste set back my introduction to Faulkner by almost fifteen years. I did not, in fact, come to terms with *Sanctuary*, actually appreciate it, feel moved by it, until I found myself—along with Horace Benbow—worrying about the safety of little Belle, until I perceived that the esential subject of *Sanctuary* was less Temple Drake than lawlessness, internal and external.

In my experience, gaining an understanding of Faulkner's women and the way in which Faulkner represents them as he does is best achieved by rereading, getting to know them better as they figure in the text of a given work. Generalizing about

Faulkner's women seems to me as fruitless as generalizing about
Faulkner's men, or about women or men in general, or about
the human race. Faulkner himself said that he did not like
generalizing about women.[3]

The best use of the present occasion, therefore, is to examine
a few of the problems that arise recurrently in relation to
Faulkner's characterization of women in hopes of throwing some
new light on the subject through scholarly investigation into
some of Faulkner's sources. Of several problems which present
themselves for consideration, I have chosen two: (1) Faulkner's
emphasis upon the physical or biological in his depiction of
women; and (2) his strong stress upon the sex drive as a
motivating force in their behavior.

The first poses what appears to be a paradox. Dr. Felix
Linder, in his reminiscence "A Gentleman of the First Order,"
has put on record Faulkner's intolerance of any vulgarities
where women were concerned. He reports that Faulkner would
not suffer a dirty joke to be told in his presence. "If somebody
started telling stories, he was gone," Dr. Linder has stated,
"whether ladies were there or I was telling or who was there." [4]
As the title of the recent book A Loving Gentleman also
emphasizes, Faulkner displayed great fastidiousness in his
intimate relationship with Meta Carpenter.[5] The general
impression which he left among those who have written about
his is that in his attitude toward women he was of the old
school—romantic, reticent, and genteel.

At the same time, critics have often charged that Faulkner's
rendering of women characters is so grossly offensive as to be

---

[3]Robert A. Jelliffe (ed.), *Faulkner at Nagano* (Tokyo: Kenkyusha, 1956), 24.
[4]James W. Webb and A. Wigfall Green (eds.), *William Faulkner of Oxford* (Baton Rouge: Louisiana State University Press, 1965), 171–73.
[5]Meta Carpenter Wilde and Orin Borsten, *A Loving Gentleman* (New York: Simon and Schuster, 1976). "He was obsessed with keeping from me the grossness of his physical self, running the water in the bathroom to cover the evidence of his animality." (p. 279)

misogynistic.[6] He has been said to depict woman only in a cow-like aspect, with emphasis upon her physical being and her reproductive capability, rather than upon her as a person with complex intellectual or emotional interests. He has been accused of giving more favorable treatment to young girls and to elderly ladies than to women in the prime of life and of being uneasy and fearful of the mature woman who is sexually available.[7]

The paradox needs resolution because—as Sally Page has observed in her book *Faulkner's Women*—an attack upon so basic an element of Faulkner's work is a challenge to the integrity of the work as a whole.[8] The paradox presents a challenge which is not to be evaded, and following William James's suggestion that one way to resolve a paradox is to make a distinction, we can attempt to distinguish between the shock effect experienced in reading the passages of Faulkner's work that are disturbing and the actual language of the texts that produce such shock. In other words, we can attempt to detach ourselves momentarily from our reactions in order to analyze Faulkner's literary craftsmanship more objectively. The effect of carrying out such a policy is to make an amazing discovery: *Faulkner is the only major American fiction writer of the twenties and thirties who incorporates into his depiction of women the functioning of the organs of reproduction.* Why this

---

[6]The best known examples of such attitudes on the part of critics are Maxwell Geismar's "William Faulkner: The Negro and the Female," in *Writers in Crisis: The American Novel between Two Wars* (Boston: Houghton Mifflin, 1942), Leslie Fiedler's analysis of Faulkner's view of women in *Love and Death in the American Novel* (New York: Criterion, 1960), and Irving Howe's *William Faulkner, A Critical Study* (New York: Random House, 1952).

[7]Albert J. Guerard, *The Triumph of the Novel* (New York: Oxford University Press, 1976). "It is . . . evident," Guerard writes, in the chapter entitled "Forbidden Games III: Faulkner's Misogyny," that "the ultimate and repugnantly forbidden game to the Faulknerian imagination was normal intercourse with a woman of marriageable age." (pp. 109–110) In a complex analysis of the relationship between the creative process and rhetorical effect, Guerard also notes Faulkner's preoccupation with cross-race sexuality and with incest, and notes elements of puritanism in his fiction even though he often exposed southern puritanism.

[8]Sally R. Page, *Faulkner's Women* (Florida: Everett/Edwards, 1972), xxii.

has not been noticed, I do not know, unless the strong taboos surrounding this subject, taboos existing even today, have blinded us to Faulkner's innovative audacity.

A more than casual artistic principle on Faulkner's part is involved; it is spelled out in *Mosquitoes*, near the close of the novel, in the scene where Fairchild stands before Gordon's completed torso of a young woman. Fairchild, with characteristic obtuseness, asks whether "a leaf or a fold of drapery" drawing "the imagination to where the organs of reproduction are concealed" would not improve the work, lending it—as the Semitic man lightly suggests—"a warmer significance." [9] The context shows that Dawson is being ridiculed because the nude torso is the embodiment of Gordon's ideal of art—and, of course, of Faulkner's as well. The nude is cold and chaste, pure as marble. It is drawn from life; it is true to life; its sexuality is neither denied nor concealed. The point of the scene in its context is that Gordon desires to depict woman the way the Greeks did their statues, in all their naturalistic nudeness, basing their representations upon an exact knowledge of female anatomy. As a writer of fiction, Faulkner naturally did not depict naked women; he rendered his women clothed, in a wide variety of costumes. But he conceived of woman as a natural, biological creature without a Christian after-the-Fall leaf or a "warmly significant" Victorian swirl of drapery.

It is unfortunate that attention to Faulkner's pejorative feminine stereotypes has not been accompanied by a recognition of the fact that his inclusion of biological data in his depictions of women renders them more accurate than those of previous male novelists. Like Whitman he saw through the drapery whether allowed to or not, thereby acknowledging the full physicality of woman, no less than that of man. His physical descriptions are never lewd or deprecatory when read in context. Examples of

---

[9]*Mosquitoes* (New York: Boni and Liveright, 1927), 321

the way he introduces the biological facts of female life into fiction for the first time (unless we regard Melville's anatomizing of the female whale as establishing a precedent) are: his reference to menstruation (when Mr. Compson counsels Quentin in *The Sound and the Fury*, and when Joe Christmas educates himself in *Light in August*); his reference to the menopause (in Joanna's missed menses in *Light in August*); his account of the process of childbirth (in Hightower's midwifery and in the convict's impromptu delivery in *The Wild Palms*); his use of such medically exact words as "uterus" and "tumescence" (in the Snopes trilogy). In *Mosquitoes*, which both announces and launches his program of naturalistic physical representation, he describes Gordon at one point as engaging in an erotic fantasy involving Pat Robyn in which the sculptor imagines himself an Israfel whose wings are "waxed by the thin odorless moisture of her thighs," [10] a biologically precise reference to the functioning of the glands of Bartholen.

A clue which helps resolve the apparent contradiction between Faulkner's personal conduct—with its niceties of reticence—and the boldness of his introduction of biological facts into his fiction, is provided by an item on Phil Stone's book order list, which was fortunately salvaged, reconstructed, and rescued from oblivion by James Meriwether.[11] The item is Dr. Louis Berman's *The Glands Regulating Personality*,[12] a volume which circumstantial evidence leads us to believe Faulkner read. However, it must always be borne in mind that, in inquiring into Faulkner's reading, we are dealing only with inferences which are drawn when Faulkner's texts are matched with similarities of wording or idea in works we think he may have read, after we have weighed the correspondences as judiciously as possible,

[10]*Ibid.*, 48.
[11]The list of Phil Stone's book purchases is included in Joseph Blotner (comp.), *William Faulkner's Library–a Catalogue* (Charlottesville, Virginia, 1964), 123–27.
[12]Louis Berman, *The Glands Regulating Personality* (New York: Macmillan, 1921).

allowing always the possibility that confluent sources may also have entered into the process of creative invention. As in exploring Shakespeare's texts through the investigation of sources that were within Shakespeare's reach, the ultimate goal is to find still more correspondences over the years, until finally we are able to arrive at the fullest possible appreciation of the synthesis that took place in Faulkner's creative imagination.

Dr. Louis Berman was a specialist in endocrinology and a theorizer like Freud or Jung who applied medical findings to human behavior in the broader sense. In the volume mentioned, he sums up and expatiates on—in highly readable fashion—the extensive medical research and theorizing on endocrinology which had made hormone therapy a subject of widespread interest in Europe and America between 1915 and 1925. In his book he systematically describes the functioning of all the ductless glands of the body, giving appropriate attention to those governing the sexual cycle in the female.

Faulkner's orientation to gland theory is evidenced in the distinction he drew between the glands and the heart in his Nobel Prize address,[13] and Berman's book therefore presents itself as one worth examining thoughtfully, both as to its general theories and its medical particulars.

Many details in Berman's book suggest themselves as having supplied specific ideas to Faulkner in his depiction of women. Of these, I shall illustrate the use of only one—a brief passage in Berman which provides a medical explanation for Joanna Burden's bizarre sexual behavior during the time of her intimate relationship with Joe Christmas. Berman, in covering the topic of menopause in the female, mentions heightened sexual desire before the climacteric in women as a phenomenon known to medical practitioners, calling it "a state of sexual hyperesthesia

---

[13]Faulkner's expression here is: ". . . not of the heart but of the glands." References to glands and hormones occur frequently throughout his work.

some women are afflicted with before the menopause." He says of this phenomenon: "It is as if the ovaries and the accessory sexual internal secretions erupt into a final geyser before they are exhausted." [14]

Faulkner, in describing the behavior of Joanna, writes of "the urgency that concealed an actual despair at frustrated and irrevocable years." He compares the waning season of Joanna's reproductive life to the changing seasons of the earth: "It was summer becoming fall, with already like shadows before a westering sun, the chill and implacable import of autumn cast ahead upon summer; something of dying summer spurting again like a dying coal in the fall." [15]

Berman, in his treatment of the reproductive cycle in women, makes it clear that the endocrines function differently during the prime of life than in youth or old age. Faulkner, we note, includes females of varying ages in many of his novels—*The Sound and the Fury*, for example, shows a complete age range, from the cradled baby daughter of Caddy to her old black nurse Dilsey. *Soldiers' Pay, Mosquitoes*, and *Sartoris* also contain women of more than one generation.

By incorporating into his characterizations an informed awareness of the differences in hormonal activity at various ages (an awareness more informed than that of his contemporaries, at any rate), Faulkner is able to do justice to the varying phases of female life: his young girls climb trees; his women in middle life cope, or fail to cope, with a complexity of yearnings and desires; his older women, like Dilsey, Rosa Millard, or Eunice Habersham, less burdened by childrearing responsibilities and less driven by internal promptings deriving from the endo-

---

[14]Berman, *The Glands Regulating Personality*, 162. Berman cites a case from literature (pp. 161–62) as an example of this disorder, naming Emma Crosby, the elderly spinster in Eugene O'Neill's *Diff'rent* as a woman who loses her emotional bearings in this way. Faulkner was, as we know, also familiar with the plays of O'Neill.
[15]*Light in August* (New York: Modern Library, 1932), 226, 228.

crines, are freer to relate integrally to the world. Within the various age-spans, however, individual women differ widely in glandular endowment. Eula Varner, for example, has an early puberty and an unusally active female hormone system, producing estrogens and progesterones in such abundance that surrounding males in the rural environment are drawn as bees to flowers.

The paradox of Faulkner's personal propriety and his literary daring, then, proves upon examination to have a simple solution: he found out what he needed to know—beyond what he could learn from observation or from experience—by reading books, the way Leonardo da Vinci studied books of anatomy in order to learn how to create his awesomely lifelike sculptures.

If Dr. Louis Berman's volume was a resource to Faulkner—as indeed it seems to have been—another work suggests itself as potentially offering still more: Dr. Havelock Ellis's monumental *Studies in the Psychology of Sex*, which appeared, in seven volumes, between the years 1897 and 1928.[16] Originally banned in England, it was published in the United States and so widely read in all parts of the world that Dr. Ellis emerges without peer as the leader of the first sexual revolution. Comprehensive and specific, Ellis's volumes were the most complete study of human sexuality available up to the publication of the Kinsey reports, exerting a direct influence upon the writings of D. H. Lawrence, James Joyce, Virgina Woolf, Henry Miller, and many others.

In order to understand how Ellis's work influenced Faulkner in his representation of women, it is not enough to examine Faulkner's derivation of small factual details from Ellis's study, though these are numerous enough. More necessary to comprehend is that Faulkner had many points of affinity with

---

[16]Faulkner mentions Ellis by name in *Mosquitoes,* in an exchange between Eva Wiseman and Fairchild, in which the former chides Fairchild for ". . . straying trustfully about this park of dark and rootless trees which Dr. Ellis and your Germans have thrown open to the public . . . ." Earlier in the same discussion, Faulkner refers to "Freud and these other—" who supply "our shelterless literati with free sleeping quarters." (pp. 248–51)

Ellis; to grasp this is to begin to perceive the intended spirituality and morality of Faulkner's approach to female sexuality. Ellis, like Faulkner, was an esthetic mystic as a young man, perceiving the world as beauty. Like Faulkner, he struggled to reconcile the physical ugliness of body facts with the exultation of spirit that derives from the stimulus of sexual desire, especially when this desire is connected with idealization of the love object. Like Faulkner, Ellis was interested in sexual modesty in all its aspects, a theme which is a source of rich humor in Faulkner, whenever he depicts a clash between the crude facts of biological life and rigidly internalized concepts which deny that life, as in "My Grandmother Millard" or "Old Man." Like Faulkner's, Ellis's approach to human sexuality was objective at the same time that it was thoroughly humane. At the root of Ellis's investigations was his desire to integrate erotic experience into fulfilling love relationships. Faulkner gives supreme value to integration of the sexual impulse into an adjusted life within the social community, as has been noted by Cleanth Brooks,[17] though Professor Brooks has arrived at this conclusion by a different route from the one I am pursuing here.

Gordon's description of the glands of Bartholen, previously mentioned, appears almost word for word as described by Ellis in *Studies in the Psychology of Sex*,[18] and evidence that Faulkner's eyes made tracks through the seven volumes is afforded by numerous parallels. Ellis, for example, made a very extensive examination of the olfactory sense as it relates to the erotic impulse. In doing so, he compared the smell of people to the smell of leaves.[19] Complexity of smell reactions analyzed by

---

[17]Cleanth Brooks, *William Faulkner: The Yoknapatawpha Country* (New Haven, Conn., 1963.)

[18]Ellis describes "a bland, more or less odorless mucous" which suffuses the vulva and vagina in tumescence. Havelock Ellis, *Studies in the Psychology of Sex* (Philadelphia: F. A. Davis Co., 1906), V, 145.

[19]Ellis, "Sexual Selection in Man," *Studies in the Psychology of Sex* (Philadelphia: F. A. Davis Co, 1911), vol. no. not specified, 63.

Ellis also figure in Faulkner's short story "Divorce in Naples," where a young sailor who is being courted by an older man rejects his homosexual advances, preferring to romanticize a waterfront prostitute, even though it is not easy for him to accept the way she smells, the hygiene of the time—it is implied—being markedly primitive. Ellis describes at length "the odor of sanctity," [20] a phrase Faulkner uses in connection with Hightower. Shoe fetishism, which Ellis calls one of the oldest and most frequent forms of erotic symbolism, [21] helps explain the consolation Benjy derives from holding Caddy's slipper and appears also in Faulkner's Indian stories. Ellis describes erotic idealization of animals, coining the word *zooerestia* to distinguish it from the cruder manifestation of bestiality, *zoophilia*, which Krafft-Ebing had catalogued as a form of antipathetic sexual instinct in his *Psychopathia Sexualis*, thus providing a source in medical annals for Ike's infatuation with his cow. [22]

Tracing such parallels as these between Ellis and Faulkner, as well as the derivations from Berman, we see that the influence of these physicians was considerable. Doubtless other medical works were also consulted by him. It is worth noting in this connection that Faulkner said his writings were read by a doctor before publication. [23]

Recognizing the extent to which medical knowledge figures in Faulkner's conception of women, we are able to place the emphasis he gives to the sex drives of women in fresh perspective. Here it is not the details, but the broader assumptions held by Berman and Ellis that are worth examining. Both physicians recognized women as possessing inherent dynamic sex energy, which is to say they saw them as sexual beings in their own right.

---

[20]*Ibid.*, 62.

[21]Ellis, *Studies in the Psychology of Sex*, V, 15–46.

[22]*Ibid.*, 77. Ellis expatiates explicitly on the difference between Krafft-Ebing's concept of *zoophilia* and his own more subjective concept, *zooerastia*.

[23]Anthony Buttita, "William Faulkner, That Writin' Man of Oxford," *Saturday Review*, XVII (May 21, 1938), 7.

Today such an idea is commonplace, but in the early years of the century, in Anglo-American culture at least, the erotic nature of woman needed first to be scientifically established, then publicized and defended. Havelock Ellis in his book *The Erotic Rights of Women* was, in fact, one of the first such defenders.[24]

Both Berman and Ellis were anti-Freudians, maintaining that Freud oversimplified, attaching too much importance to the sex drives as such and ignoring other factors. Faulkner was anti-Freudian also, objecting to Freudian dream analysis and to the procedure of psychoanalysis.[25] Berman explained human behavior primarily in terms of body chemistry, viewing the glands as triggering the body mechanisms and influencing brain functioning.[26] The commanding role of the rational faculties in man, he maintained, was, to a considerable extent, a misconception. The brain, in Berman's opinion, did not direct the body; rather, it was in the service of the body. Drives produced by the endocrines influenced the brain. A disordered endocrine system caused mental distortion and mad behavior.[27]

---

[24]Havelock Ellis, *The Erotic Rights of Women, and the Objects of Marriage* (London: Battley Bros,. 1918). See also Ellis's *Little Essays of Love and Virtue* (New York: G. H. Doran Co., 1922).

[25]See in Carvel Collins (ed.), *William Faulkner: Early Prose and Poetry* (Boston: Little, Brown and Co., 1962), "Books and Things," in which Faulkner writes: "Writing people are all so pathetically torn between a desire to make a figure in the world and a morbid interest in their personal egos—the deadly fruit of the grafting of Sigmund Freud upon the dynamic chaos of a hodge-podge of nationalities." He describes Robert Edmund Jones's use of "the new therapeutic psycho-analysis" and observes that the tendency to be "siked" is one of the things that modern writers must "combat," remarking that "so long as socialism, psycho-analysis, and the aesthetic attitude are profitable as well as popular, so long will [the prevailing adverse cultural conditions] obtain." (pp. 93–94) Also revealing of Faulkner's attitude towards Freud is a comment on the side of a letter from Natalie Scott to Faulkner written October 29, 1928, to Lyle Saxon: "Tell Bill Faulkner I dreamed about him the other night! Nothing Freudian (if he is uneasy)." Mss. Archives, Tulane University. Cited with permission of Tulane University Library.

[26]Berman, *The Glands Regulating Personality*, 165–85.

[27]The view that man functions primarily through the nervous system, rather than through the intellect, is also elaborated by Berman in *The Personal Equation* (New York: Century Co., 1925). Here Berman posits the interesting idea of what he calls the "psychico-chemical person," as an aspect of the human being which is basic and which should be considered equally with the "ancestral person" and the "historical person." (p. 33)

Such an emphasis accords well with the sense of determinism which pervades Faulkner's writing. It explains, in medical terms, the terrifying apprehension his characters experience when they feel themselves driven, compelled, in the grip of forces they cannot master, forces from within intermeshing with forces from without—with no possibility of control. Here we have an explanation for the terrifying actions of such frustrated women as Emily Grierson, Minnie Cooper, Zilphia Gant, and others, whose compulsive behavior is rooted in a repressed sex drive. Mental distortion keeps them from having a rational perception of their own actions. A tragic relentlessness sets in when their impulses connect with socially determined impulses in the world around them, impulses which have a momentum of their own because they derive from history. Impulses deriving from religious puritanism and from social decadence are conspicuously evident. Faulkner's most perturbed women, like Temple Drake, Narcissa, Drusilla, and Emily Grierson, thus express in their behavior both their own thwarted or perverted drives and those aspects of their culture which, in Faulkner's view, were the least wholesome—prudery, class snobbery, arrogant racism.

Among other general ideas held by Ellis and Berman which are illuminating in relation to Faulkner's depiction of women is that the distinction between masculine and feminine in human beings is not as sharp as is often assumed. Ellis speaks of "the latent bisexuality of each sex"; Berman maintains that "biologically there exists every transition between the masculine and the feminine." [28]

Faulkner's interest in the ambiguities of sex differentiation appears first overtly in *Mosquitoes*, where he includes among his cast of characters a set of twins of college age, Josh and Pat. Josh,

---

[28]Havelock Ellis, *Man and Woman, a Study of Human Secondary Sexual Characteristics* (6th ed.; London: A. B. C. Black, 1926), 317; Berman, *The Glands Regulating Personality*, 134.

the boy, is broodingly creative; Pat, the girl, is a tomboy. In the same novel a languidly feminine young woman, Jennie, is sexually arousing to both men and women. Eva Wiseman in *Mosquitoes*—her name obviously embodying both sexes— writes a poem entitled "Hermaphroditus," which later appears in *The Green Bough* as one of Faulkner's own.

A line from Théophile Gautier's *Mademoiselle de Maupin*, a book in which there is as much shifting of sex roles as in Shakespeare's *As You Like It*, is introduced into the text of the novel.[29] It would appear that Faulkner, like Shakespeare, arrived early at an awareness of the androgyny of the creative mind, as well as a perception of the infinite shadings of the masculine and feminine in human beings. As Sally Page has noted, many of his women have personality traits often called masculine—Mannie Hait's physical rage in *Mule in the Yard*, Drusilla's soldierly courage in *The Unvanquished*, and Charlotte Rittenmeyer's sexual aggressiveness, to name a few.[30] Also not to be omitted in any consideration of Faulkner's characters of dubious sexuality are those darlings of his heart, his charming boy-girls, the slim-hipped Venuses who had been erotically idealized for him—fatefully, it would appear—by his early poetic mentors, Verlaine and Swinburne.

When Faulkner said it was "more fun" to write about women characters than about men, he added also that it was "more difficult." He knew, he said, "so little about them." [31] By this remark he expresses, to my view, two significant attitudes. The first is all too rarely found in contemporary American literature by male writers—the ability to perceive women not as mere projections of themselves, but as human beings in their own

---

[29]Théophile Gautier, *Mademoiselle de Maupin* (Paris, 1879), 211. "Trois choses me plaisent: l'or, le marbre et la Pourpe, éclat, solidité, couleur," appears in the Semitic Man's statement at the close, pp. 338–40: "I love three things: gold, marble and purple . . .—form solidity color."

[30]Page, *Faulkner's Women*, 11–135, 178–79.

[31]Gwynn and Blotner, (eds.) *Faulkner in the University*, 45.

right, separate and distinct. The second expresses his desire to work from objective knowledge, from medically validated information that is accurate, reliable, up-to-date. What is impressive here is that he did more than seek knowledge; he saw to it that those elemental facts of biological life which prudery in his day commanded be expunged were deliberately incorporated. Hemingway and Sinclair Lewis, both sons of physicians and amply knowledgeable, knuckled under to Mrs. Grundy. Faulkner did not.

His inclusion of the physiological in his characterization of women affects the overall interpretation of his work in unexpected, extremely important ways. As almost every reader has discovered, one of the characteristics of Faulkner's work is its capacity to lend itself to an unusually large number of interpretations, almost like human experience itself. His inclusion of the biological significantly increases the possiblities of such multi-level interpretation. Because they are complete physiological entities, Faulkner's women may readily be construed as archetypes, for example. Or, they can effectively personify mythical women—Eve, Io, Persephone, Diana, Venus, or others—thereby making themselves available for a sexual interpretation of history. Or they can be viewed—as Cleanth Brooks has done—as social beings living in a given time or place, stereotypes of the clearly differentiated social roles of women in an old-fashioned society. Or, they can serve to reflect the larger prevailing patterns of social organization in the modern world. As such, they support Faulkner's goal of writing works that would not be injured by translation,[32] for even though sexual mores have been in a process of rapid change in the twentieth century, erotic love in Western society—as in most of the rest of the world—is still legitimatized only within the family

---

[32]*Mosquitoes*, 243. The reference to works which "translation will not injure" seems to express an ideal of Faulkner's own.

structure. Furthermore, the biological element, however much it may be transcended by woman in her mental activity or her work, constitutes a fundamental point of identification among women. It is shared by all—regardless of nationality, race, or skin color.

It cannot be denied that Faulkner's vision, which encompasses the supernally lovely and the bestial, the tremulously yearning and the most brutally violent, includes women characters as objects and women characters as agents. In the *Divine Comedy* of Faulkner's creation, women appear in every part—in his *Paradiso*, in his *Inferno*, and in his *Purgatorio*. Nor can it be gainsayed that the eyes which perceive imaginative reality in Faulkner's work are masculine eyes, belonging to a man of epical ambition, one who strives for Homer's gift of narration, Spenser's rhetorical lushness, and Milton's loftiness of purpose. As Charles Olson once observed, there are always only two eyes looking;[33] in Faulkner's work, those eyes are undeniably the eyes of a man.

What a probing of two of his medical sources here shows is that he was far more modern than we have allowed, far more audacious than we have perceived, far more reverential of human life as it manifests itself in woman than we have credited.

---

[33]"Letter 6," *The Maximus Poems* (New York: Jargon/Corinth Books, 1960), 29. The exact quotation is: "There are no hierarchies, no infinite, no such many as mass, there are only/eyes in all heads,/to be looked out of"/.

Faulkner & Race

MARGARET WALKER ALEXANDER

William Faulkner's greatness may well be his unique achievement in incorporating the American myth about race and the
Christian myth of redemption in a body of fiction that is symbolic, humanistic, timeless, and universal. He successfully
communicates to his readers a sense of history combined with a
deep-seated sense of morality or honor. His vision is tragi-comic
and his tradition is truly that of American Gothic. His use of
symbol, myth, and legend is indisputably great. He is the only
white American whose use of race and religion in literature can
be said to plumb the depths of myth which, of course, is the
seedbed of both religion and literature.

Race in Faulkner's fiction is not limited to one racial group.
He deals with three races in his native state—the red man who
was here first, the white man whose threefold guilt obsesses
him, and the black man who is a pawn, a type, a shapeless
symbol, a victim or scapegoat, and who only occasionally
achieves humanity. One must read a large body of Faulkner's
fiction from the beginning to the end in order to understand
even slightly his strange code of honor, his attitude about race,
and his deeply religious commitment. Yet this morality, or
moral concern about race, is stamped on every major work and is
especially thematic in the big body of his fiction. Some smaller
pieces are even more perfected forms of this interest. "That
Evening Sun" is notable but the entire early collection *Go*

Down, Moses deals with Faulkner's Negroes. Dilsey in *The Sound and the Fury*, Lucas Beauchamp in *Intruder in the Dust*, and Joe Christmas in *Light in August* are important racial characters. In "The Old People," "Red Leaves," and "The Bear," Faulkner emphasizes the Indians, but here there are also black and white as well as red people.

The racial theme may best be understood in terms of the original Cain-Abel conflict, "Am I my brother's keeper?" Faulkner's symbol for southern society—and in time all society, for universal man and for his condition is the man of mixed blood. In his early work these characters—and there are a number of them—are at war with self. The mulatto is a symbol for the problem of race relations—brother's abuse of brother—man against man.

The universal man or Christ figure seen in earlier novels is exemplified by Joe Christmas of *Light in August* and Charles Bon of *Absalom, Absalom!* But in *Go Down, Moses*, particularly in "The Bear," distinctions are made.

Boon is a man of mixed blood; white-Indian is a symbol of the spirit of the frontier and of the property consciousness of the white man because Boon's blood has run white. Boon is a symbol of frustration—the last picture of him objectifies the consequence of this.

But Sam Fathers—whom McCaslin Edmonds thinks of as a tragic mulatto, a man at war within himself—is not tragic at all. He is really a man at peace. In him (he is half Indian and half Negro) the blood has run black. He is humble before nature—he is the only fit tutor for Ike. It is he who teaches Ike what he needs to know to free himself from the curse on Israel—"Sam Fathers Set Me Free," Ike tells McCaslin Edmonds.[1]

Another mulatto—Lucas Beauchamp, descendant of Carothers McCaslin through the Negro line—is described this way

---

[1]"The Bear."

in "The Fire and the Hearth": "and if this is what that McCaslin blood has brought me I don't want it neither, and if the running of it into my black blood never hurt him any more than the running of it out is going to hurt me, it wont even be old Carothers that had the most pleasure." [2]

The experience of discovering the source of the curse and his responsibility for it stimulates Ike to act. This he does as step by step he progresses backward beyond "was," beyond his father's and uncle's world. To identify the first sin. To see his grandfather, Carothers McCaslin, as his grandfather really was. He discovers there the sin. Not the miscegenation—perish the thought—but the incest and that not because it is incest but because this act, the use of his own daughter as a thing for his pleasure rather than as daughter or even as human being, violates her humanity in the most crass way Faulkner can imagine.

Buck and Buddy feel the guilt and they increase the legacy—the legacy of man's crime against his fellowman. Ike, even here, finally recognizes that this is not just his grandfather's sin: "until at last He saw that they were all Grandfather all of them and that from even the best." [3]

Black students and even some whites who read "The Bear" may be bothered by some things in it that they see as racist. Faulkner was, in fact, a racist—but two or three things are important to note. First of all, he knew that and knew it thirty-five or forty years before anyone much talked in such terms. Secondly, and I will comment more fully on all these things later, he knew that the whole of American society in these United States—North and South—was racist. Thirdly, he moved beyond where many people are today to discover that in an important way, to say one is a racist is to say one is human and the product of his culture. And, fourthly, and finally, and more

---

[2] "The Fire and the Hearth," in *Go Down, Moses* (Vintage ed.), 57.
[3] "Was," in *Go Down, Moses*.

importantly, he did not conclude that this realization (that is to be racist is to be human) removed any of the guilt and responsibility from the perceiver. For Faulkner devoted a good share of his work, his ability, to the problem of coming to terms with his racism (in a social context). Learning this, and attempting to do something about it, is what "The Bear" is all about, particularly part five. Here there is a redefinition of myth.

Faulkner's philosophy has often seemed puzzling and in the early years of his career must have been completely misunderstood, certainly by those few critics who first judged him as a Communist, a Socialist realist, or a naturalist such as Granville Hicks and, even later, by the New Critics from the Ivy League who began to read everything in terms of the Christian myth of redemption, pointing out epiphany, baptism, transfiguration, crucifixion, and resurrection in every Faulkner product. Faulkner has been treated as stoic humanist, Christian, and segregationist—the three are not necessarily compatible. For our purposes here Faulkner is a symbolist treating characters as symbols and types, preferring to deal with the standards of life as human rather than divine or bestial, hating always the nonhuman, the mechanical, or mechanistic, and believing always in the human spirit, the human being, the human heart. Faulkner should be read as one reads the Bible—not literally but figuratively.

Whether his characters are red, black, or white they symbolize certain basic ideas, social classes, racial types, codes of honor, and traditional versus nontraditional standards or values. They are therefore symbols. Individuation and characters in the round may rarely be found in Faulkner. He is not concerned with delineating or developing character. Rather he reveals their shadowy shapes and even the names he gives them are symbolic: Nancy Mannigoe—she goes with many men; Lena Grove—the nature symbol, of a tree; Candace or Candy—sweet and sexually seductive; The Snopeses—snooping and like swine, a pig's (snope) snout; Jesus—the black cuckold husband of Nancy in "That Evening Sun"; Joe Christmas—the tragic mulatto and Christ figure.

Despite Faulkner's admission that demons drove him, we understand his complex genius as intuitive, insightful, and brooding, thoughtful genius together with the demonic and the orphic. We can thus begin to understand how the great welter of his imagination and his chief frame of reference must be his own family history, his familiar home surroundings, the people of his own town and county. What he called his postage stamp or world in microcosm.

Just as Yoknapatawpha is not merely a creation or figment of his own imagination but in reality the country he has known all his life, his characters are, too, the same familiar people he has known in that country. The red men must be the same red men he has either known or been accustomed to conceiving as such—as hunters, brave and courageous and men initiated into manhood through bravery and courage. The black men are the menials or servant Negroes he has known, the suffering servants as in Isaiah, the prophet; the whites, rich and poor, are his own family and neighbors. Real and legendary, they do not come from another country.

If we first define the American myth about race and later explain the religious myth of Christian redemption as seen in Faulkner, we can perhaps understand the magnitude of his achievement.

Faulkner was born into a southern USA community in Mississippi where racial attitudes, mores, and customs had crystallized into a pattern of social behavior for at least a hundred years. He was born into a racially segregated society and all of his life he must have been a segregationist.

The American myth about race is built around an idea of racial superiority and inferiority. The master race is superior to the slave race in such a philosophy. The slave race is not comprised of adult human beings but childlike, animal-like creatures who are seen possessing certain typical characteristics. In such a conceived body of thought the red man and black man are primitives, untouched by the corrupting taint of civilization—savages but noble beings, nevertheless, born with natural honor and integrity. The civilized white man, however, is not a primitive, that is, he is not innocent. He has tasted the fruit of the tree of knowledge, of good and evil, and he is guilty of the sin of disobedience and is doomed to death. His guilt or sin is threefold in Faulknerian terms. He has sinned against nature or the land by abusing it; he has sinned against the red man by usurping his land and annihilating his people; and he has sinned against the black man not only by enslaving him but has stooped to the unpardonable sin of miscegenation by violating black women and thus has brought the mixed breed or mongrelized race of mixed blood into existence. These are the sins or crimes between the white man and God. He has therefore lost honor and integrity and he is damned to the fires of hell. This should not be called merely a southern myth. It belongs to all white America and is as old as the nation itself.

Now, I must hasten to add that white Americans believing this myth are not aware that it is a myth nor how it became one. But how it became a myth is beside the point. This is the myth about race that Faulkner grew up hearing, believing, and having ingrained into him. His rational powers of thought may have questioned all the nuances of this racial rationalization or rationale for slavery and segregation, but as he says, "memory believes before knowing remembers." Some critics offer an interesting theory of how Faulkner's fiction follows a line of growing awareness of humanity in the black man.

Faulkner was not only born white in a segregated society comprised of three races—two regarded as inferior and one as superior—he was born in the Bible Belt where Christian honor, virtue, and integrity were standards accepted as ideal and perfect. Faulkner is therefore white segregationist and southern Christian. He is very much like the puritan Hawthorne in this respect. It has already been pointed out how Faulkner can be compared with many other great American novelists—Mark Twain and Nathaniel Hawthorne for example. His first book, *The Marble Faun*, shows how Hawthorne influenced Faulkner. He is also deeply influenced by fundamentalism in religion, and the Protestant or Calvinist obsession with sin. Beginning with the Pentateuch or Torah, the entrance of evil or sin and death into the world, the ideas of sacrifice from Abraham and Isaac to the New Testament of Jesus Christ as the Lamb of God—the whole story of sin and redemption may be seen transposed and sublimated into Faulkner's fiction. All-men-are-brothers-and-God-is-our-Father is an idea negated by racism or segregationist views of religion, of man, and God. A myth about race is absolutely necessary for such inherent contradictions in the society in order to mitigate them.

Dilsey, Beauchamp, Joe Christmas, and Nancy Mannigoe are all tied to the myth of Christian redemption as surely as they are victims of the racial myth and segregated society. But Faulkner is quick to advance the theory that only in the racially mixed such as Joe Christmas is there tragic conflict. Earlier, Sherwood Anderson was amazed that Faulkner believes an old wives' tale that mulattoes are hybrids like mules and cannot reproduce. If Faulkner was pulling his leg, Anderson never realized it. Joe Christmas suffers because he lacks racial identity and his tragedy is therefore the tragedy of miscegenation or mixed blood.

But the honor of Faulkner's house of heroes or anti-heroes is the honor of Christian integrity, an integrity violated by a breach of five of the ten commandments: Thou shalt not steal; Thou shalt not kill; Thou shalt not commit adultery; Thou shalt not covet; Thou shalt not bear false witness, or Thou shalt not lie. But drunkenness, lying, incest, murder, rape, and swearing or

111

cursing great oaths—all these are prevalent in the violent, Gothic, macabre atmosphere of Faulknerian fiction. Love, honor, integrity, reverence are not merely Old Testament commandments. These are Christian virtues.

The moral problem is therefore central in Faulkner. The moral problem of race is just as central as the religious problem of sin and redemption. The problem of evil is both the problem of sin and the shadow of race. And the two are constantly intertwined. Class is also very important to Faulkner. Quality white folks are not as dirty and low-down as low class white folks. Old man Sutpen and the Snopeses are not in the same class with Colonel Sartoris because they stooped to actions only inferior men would stoop to do, such as taking the so-called "wild" Negroes from Africa and beating them down into submission and cheap labor as slaves in order to build plantations, estates, and material empires. Then as if this were not enough, compounded with the evil of slavery is the evil of miscegenation. Stooping to black women is not only a racial sin but a sin against class and honor. Lynching and rape and miscegenation do not touch the garments of the rich until the whole white South is cursed by slavery. And then after the Civil War, decadence begins. Even the Compsons are cursed with cupidity because of sexual greed and greed for money. These are the evil fruits of slavery. "Radix Malorum est Cupiditas," the root of evil is desire.

There are a number of superficial facts about race in Faulkner. One is his use and understanding of Negro folklore, such as the spiritual "Go Down, Moses," lynching, and the title from Handy's St. Louis Blues, "That Evening Sun"—the various symbolic meanings of blood: washed in the blood of the Lamb—blood from the deer—on the boy's forehead as an initiation rite—the classic belief of low comedy in the role of class and subculture.

Dilsey and Joe Christmas are frequently cited as Faulkner's greatest black characters—but if you ask black people they would choose Lucas Beauchamp in *Intruder in the Dust*. Here for the first time in Faulkner is a black man with dignity, one who approaches if not achieves humanity. Dilsey is a type, and Christmas is a symbol, but Beauchamp is almost a man. Dilsey as a character is a flat, mindless stereotype. She is in the plantation tradition established by John Pendleton Kennedy's *Swallow Barn*. As a mammy, a faithful old retainer, she is unacceptable to the average black reader as a real black mother. It is one thing for her white folks to love her and for her to love their children—this is a carryover from the economic system of slavery—but it is utterly unnatural for her to mistreat her own child at the same time by calling him a fool. As a deeply religious person, fundamentalist in her faith, she would fear hell-fire for calling anyone a fool. Because she is a domestic servant, because she is a menial, because she is a type, it is in the typical fashion of white American tradition to invest her with love, compassion, pity, and bravery. This is Faulkner's use of character in the traditional fashion. Perhaps he is influenced by his love for his own mammy, Caroline Barr. Perhaps the character of Dilsey is modeled after her and surely Faulkner felt deep affection for her as he must have felt she showed him love and kindness, genuine and sincerely felt; but insofar as greatness of being is concerned, Dilsey does not qualify as a great character merely because she was a servant. And she certainly wasn't humble. She not only ran her family and the Compsons—she *knew* she kept them together and she knew she was the boss.

"Oh, Lawd," Dilsey said. She set the sifter down and swept up the hem of her apron and wiped her hands and caught up the bottle from the chair on which she had laid it and gathered her apron about the handle of the kettle which was now jetting faintly. "Jes a minute," she called, "De water jes dis minute got hot."

It was not the bottle which Mrs. Compson wanted however, and clutching it by the neck like a dead hen Dilsey went to the foot of the stairs and looked upward.

113

"Aint Luster up dar wid him?" she said.

"Luster hasn't been in the house. I've been lying here listening for him. I knew he would be late, but I did hope he'd come in time to keep Benjamin from disturbing Jason on Jason's one day in the week to sleep in the morning."

"I dont see how you expect anybody to sleep, wid you standin in de hall, holl'in at folks fum de crack of dawn," Dilsey said. She began to mount the stairs, toiling heavily. "I sont dat boy up dar half hour ago."

Mrs. Compson watched her, holding the dressing gown under her chin. "What are you going to do?" she said.

"Gwine git Benjy dressed en bring him down to de kitchen, whar he wont wake Jason en Quentin," Dilsey said.

"Haven't you started breakfast yet?"

"I'll tend to dat too," Dilsey said. "You better git back in bed twell Luster make yo fire. Hit cold dis mawnin."

"I know it," Mrs. Compson said. "My feet are like ice. They were so cold they waked me up." She watched Dilsey mount the stairs. It took her a long while. "You know how it frets Jason when breakfast is late," Mrs. Compson said.

"I cant do but one thing at a time," Dilsey said. "You git on back to bed, fo I has you on my hands dis mawnin too."

"If you're going to drop everything to dress Benjamin, I'd better come down and get breakfast. You know as well as I do how Jason acts when it's late."

"En who gwine eat yo messin?" Dilsey said. "Tell me dat. Go on now," she said, toiling upward. Mrs. Compson stood watching her as she mounted, steadying herself against the wall with one hand, holding her skirts up with the other.[4]

There is no question in my mind but that Faulkner progresses in his understanding of black humanity as portrayed in his fictional characters who are black. His black trilogy really consists of *Light in August*, first published in 1932, followed by *Go Down, Moses* ten years later in 1942, and concludes with *Intruder in the Dust* in 1948. This last novel comes twenty-two years after his first novel, *Soldiers' Pay*, and a little over a

---

[4]*The Sound and the Fury* (Modern Library ed.), 286–87.

year before he won the Nobel Prize. The two major characters concerned with race are Joe Christmas, who really does not know who he is and therein lies his tragedy—loss of identity, and alienation—and Lucas Beauchamp, who grows as a character in Faulkner's mind over some fourteen or fifteen years. Lucas is the only one of Faulkner's black characters who approaches or approximates a man. He almost never begs the question of his humanity as Jesus' wife Nancy does when she says "It's not my fault. I ain't nothing but a nigger." [5] Lucas repeatedly asserts his manhood. He not only asserts it, he maintains it and acts with the dignity he feels befitting his manhood. The tragic figure in "Pantaloon in Black" is exactly as Faulkner describes him, a clown, a buffoon, the typical minstrel type he is. He reminds us of the great Pagliacci. "Laugh clown laugh," even when your heart is breaking. The minstrel type, clown or buffoon, is exemplified in Rider of "Pantaloon in Black."

"So Ketcham come on back down stairs and pretty soon the chain gang come in and went on up to the bull pen and he thought things had settled down for a while when all of a sudden he begun to hear the yelling, not howling: yelling, though there wasn't no words in it, and he grabbed his pistol and run back up stairs to the bull pen where the chain gang was and Ketcham could see into the cell where the old woman was kind of squinched down in one corner and where that nigger had done tore that iron cot clean out of the floor it was bolted to and was standing in the middle of the cell, holding the cot over his head like it was a baby's cradle, yelling, and says to the old woman, 'Ah aint goan hurt you,' and throws the cot against the wall and comes and grabs holt of that steel barred door and rips it out of the wall, bricks, hinges and all, and walks out of the cell toting the door over his head like it was a gauze window screen, hollering, 'It's awright. It's awright. Ah aint trying to git away.'

"Of course Ketcham could have shot him right there, but like he

---

[5] "That Evening Sun," in *Collected Stories* (Vintage ed.), 293.

said, if it wasn't going to be the law, then them Birdsong boys ought to have the first lick at him. So Ketcham dont shoot. Instead, he jumps in behind where them chain gang niggers was kind of backed off from that steel door, hollering, 'Grab him! Throw him down!' except the niggers hung back at first too until Ketcham gets in where he can kick the ones he can reach, batting at the others with the flat of the pistol until they rush him. And Ketcham says that for a full minute that nigger would grab them as they come in and fling them clean across the room like they was rag dolls, saying, 'Ah aint trying to git out. Ah aint tryin to git out,' until at last they pulled him down—a big mass of nigger heads and arms and legs boiling around on the floor and even then Ketcham says every now and then a nigger would come flying out and go sailing through the air across the room, spraddled out like a flying squirrel and with his eyes sticking out like car headlights, until at last they had him down and Ketcham went in and begun peeling away niggers until he could see him laying there under the pile of them, laughing, with tears big as glass marbles running across his face and down past his ears and making a kind of popping sound on the floor like somebody dropping bird eggs, laughing and laughing and saying, 'Hit look lack Ah just cant quit thinking. Look lack Ah just cant quit.' And what do you think of that?"

"I think if you eat any supper in this house you'll do it in the next five minutes," his wife said from the dining room. "I'm going to clear this table then and I'm going to the picture show." [6]

So then, Faulkner runs the gamut to traditional and nontraditional treatment of black characters. Blacks are equated first with animals—" 'Them damn niggers,' he said. 'I swear to godfrey, it's a wonder we have as little trouble with them as we do. Because why? Because they aint human. They look like a man and they walk on their hind legs like a man, and they can talk and you can understand them and you think they are understanding you, at least now and then. But when it comes to the normal human feelings and sentiments of human beings, they might just as well be a damn herd of wild buffaloes' " [7]—

[6]"Pantaloon in Black," in Go Down, Moses (Vintage ed.), 158–59.
[7]Ibid., 154.

considered wild savages, then children, then as stereotypes, then as clowns or buffoons, and only in Lucas Beauchamp does a black man approach humanity. "I'm a nigger," Lucas said, "but I'm a man too." [8]

Faulkner tries to avoid the old stereotypes about race brought over from the plantation tradition, even though quite unconsciously he changes some of these old stereotypes into new stereotypes. He rejects the idea that all Negroes are lazy, steal, are nasty, and that they are always raping white people. Faulkner's Negroes are more often victims of poor and lower-class Caucasians who are not above rape, murder, incest, and all such crimes of greed and passion. He maintains, however, most of the sexual stereotypes and taboos that have racial labels. He clings to the plantation ideas and stereotypes of the faithful old retainer, the black wet nurse, the mammy, the kind of Negro that Dilsey is. He invests her with dignity, love, compassion, and above all the ability to endure and survive the outrage of slavery, servitude, and segregation. He either knows no educated blacks or has no respect for them. He regards the Negro's adjustment and adaptability to Western white world culture as superior to the inscrutable primitivism of the Indian or red man who insists on clinging to all the old ways of his dying culture and annihilated civilization. Faulkner does not accept any part of the red man's integration or amalgamation into white American society which is, nevertheless, a definite though little known fact. Sam Fathers is a symbol of the past and an old culture. His name is a typical symbol. The Indians in Faulkner symbolize an inscrutable, mysterious folk culture completely foreign to the white man. The black man (he thinks he understands) he can either relate to, condescend toward, or pointedly ignore when it suits his purpose. He can insult his blackness by treating him as if he were invisible. But the red man is outside the pale of his mercy,

---

[8]"The Fire and the Hearth," in *Go Down, Moses*, 47.

beyond his understanding, and not a clear or coherent part of either his myth about race or his myth about religion. The white man's guilt toward the red man overwhelms him and he cannot deal rationally with this guilt. In "Red Leaves," "The Bear," and "Was," Faulkner presents us with the red man as part of the great wilderness, totally a part of nature, having integrity only as long as he keeps himself inviolate, free of slavery and miscegenation. When the Indian buys slaves and and mixes with black women, as Sam Fathers is the result of (his mother was a black slave and his father a Chickasaw chief), then the Indian's sin is the same as the white man's. He grows weaker and dies or becomes extinct. But this is not really the reason for the extinction of the red man as we very well know. The red man lost the military battle and war with the white man, but disease was really the white man's tool used to destroy the red man. It was the red man who was massacred into extinction. He is ambivalent and outside the white man's moral code. Faulkner extols the ideal of racial purity or integrity regardless of the particular color, red, white, and black.

Sam Fathers is the pathetic, tragic mixed man, red and black, yet he seems not to be disturbed either by pathos or tragedy.

"The Bear" is therefore the best example of Faulkner's fiction in which the symbolic significance of his three races—red, white, and black—is carefully interwoven so that theme, action, character, and style are all of one piece. Many teachers and authorities agree that the shorter piece and original "Bear" is a better short story—technically speaking. But in the longer piece the racial ideas, myth, and theme can be seen as giving rise to morality, honor, comments on time, and in general expressing Faulkner's Weltanschauung—philosophy and world view.

In Faulkner's world or "system" that he consciously makes, the worlds of the Old and New Testaments are melded into a myth that accommodates the American myth about race and sees man in an almost fatalistic sense, only ameliorated by his faith in man's spirit—man's heart—man's living soul—a humanism which he says will in the end against all odds prevail.

The student of southern literature must constantly be confronted with the problem of race; Race has been an issue in the literature from the beginning of southern literature and history. Most of us have studied this literature and history as we have observed and been part of the culture. Because of the nature of more than three hundred years of southern history, the student of American literature tends to think only in terms of the achievements of one race; and because of the nature of the two institutions of slavery and segregation, the issue of racism in the literature has only recently been considered. The history and the literature of the region are a reflection of the life and culture of the people. Therefore we encounter racial characters, themes, philosophy, and the southern scene in all of southern literature. The themes of violence and decadence are as natural in Faulkner as in any other American literature. But Faulkner represents the first real breakthrough in American literature on the treatment of race, both in terms of philosophy and in terms of technique. He follows here the tradition of Melville and Hawthorne. Faulkner considers all classes and all races in his native Mississippi. He is familiar with all the hackneyed themes of miscegenation and the tragic mulatto. He deals with the southern landscape in a meaningful fashion, and as a symbolist he creates a fictitious world that thoroughly absorbs the American myth about race. Polarity in Faulkner means the juxtaposition of race against race, class against class, reality and imagination, symbolism and realism, verisimilitude. In Faulkner we see for the first time the southern white writer rising above time and place, struggling beyond the racist limitations of his society into the truly rarified world of the artist, a world in which human values and universal truths take precedence over the provincial and philistine notions of bigoted minds. Like all great writers in the world he moves from the local to the universal, from the

119

immediate to the timeless, and from the simple into the sublime. It is toward this idealistic goal that we must all strive. If we cannot dream with the great mythic imagination of Faulkner we can at least aspire toward the splendid failure of his dream.

Perhaps the single most glaring fault black Americans find with southern literature by white writers is in the psychology and philosophy which of necessity in most instances is racist. This has to be understood in terms of the society, the values emphasized in American education, the nature of slavery and segregation which not only have kept the races apart, separated, and polarized in two segregated societies but have ostracized the scholarly and artistic achievements or accomplishments of black people and ignored their literature. The white and racist scholar has been educated not to accept the intellectual capacity of the black man. A thinking being is unacceptable as a slave. Creativity? The earliest writers, black and white, were fighting a racial battle; the white writers were writing apologies for slavery, and the black writers were protesting against the inhumanity of the slave system. Slavery as an economic system was part of the rise of capitalism, and Christianity in the institutionalized church or religion became the tool of capitalism as a Western world religion. Segregation was a substitution for slavery. Under segregation the white child was educated to regard race as more important than common humanity and the black child was taught to hate himself and to imitate a white world as superior to his. The battle and the conflict can be seen in the literature. Thomas Wolfe went far from home but he never outgrew his racial prejudices. Reading Mark Twain's stories as a child I came across the word "nigger" and put the book down. Years later hearing the ironic incident told as a joke I could not laugh: "Heard about a terrible accident," and one asked, "Did anybody get hurt?" "Nome, just killed a nigger." The full implication was that a black man was not a human being and this was the racist problem of early southern literature. But it is also important to relate here that by the same token much of American literature outside the South did not move me at all. If the South seemed obsessed by race at least it was a subject. For that same reason Hemingway's fiction to me is certainly not as immediate and meaningful as Faulkner's.

The South is not alone guilty in terms of racism. All America today suffers from the sickness of racism. All America today also suffers from paranoia. White America seems to have the strange sickness of delusions of grandeur and a god-complex, while black Americans seem to suffer from delusions of persecution, not without some factual basis. None of us is willing to believe any of it is only a delusion. But our literature reflects our society; when we are a polarized or segregated society, our literature is also. We would hope for a healing of our sick society, sick of war and division, sick of material values and a quality of life gone sour with pollution, with militarism, racism, and materialism. Our hope for the future must be with the proverbial madmen of the world, the priests and the poets, and the lovers.[9] All of them are mad, drunk with love and religion and the smoke of inspiration. But the artists have always been, too, the *avant garde*. They have the ideas which the philosophers generate and they implement the new concepts of the universe in order that man may build a better society. It is therefore in the literature of today that we have hope for cultural change tomorrow. Literature is a cultural instrument and as such we build toward a new twenty-first century that will have learned all the sad lessons of the twentieth century. Perhaps we will produce together all that is needed for one race on the face of the earth, the human race. Surely William Faulkner has made a great beginning.

---

[9] Plato, *The Phaedrus.*

Yoknapatawpha & Faulkner's Fable of Civilization

LEWIS P. SIMPSON

In this second discussion I want to treat in a somewhat more comprehensive way the big, complex, and subtle topic I attempted to approach earlier in my remarks on sex and history in Faulkner's writings, that is to say, his perspective on history and civilization.[1] My remarks will regard three aspects of his outlook. I shall briefly comment on what I have come to term the subject of the modern novel. I will define this as the myth of the past in the present, or the literary myth of modern history; and I will point out the relation of this myth to the American literary consciousness. In this connection I shall also point out that Faulkner's version, or vision, of the novelistic subject includes not only the myth of the past in the present but the loss of this myth, together with the threatened loss of the very capacity of the imagination to make mythic constructs of existence. Finally I shall observe that as, under pressure of his vision of the myth of the past in the present, Faulkner invents a highly particularized myth of history, Yoknapatawpha County, he implies a larger myth of man. In remarking on the larger myth—which struggles to emerge out of the Yoknapatawpha

---

[1]See Simpson's "Sex and History: Origins of Faulkner's Apocyp" in this volume, pp. 43–70.

myth but is never clearly articulated—I will attempt briefly to consider the meaning of Faulkner's largest non-Yoknapatawpha work, *A Fable*, in what I conceive as its crucial, pivotal relation to the Yoknapatawpha stories.

The source of my concept of the literary myth of modern history and its bearing on the southern novel is one which I have often quoted and which I share in common with every student of southern letters. This is Allen Tate's recognition of the signficance of twentieth-century southern fiction in "The Profession of Letters in the South" (1935):

> The Southern novelist has left his mark upon the age; but it is of the age. From the peculiarly historical consciousness of the Southern writer has come good work of a special order; but the focus of this consciousness is quite temporary. It has made possible the curious burst of intelligence that we get at a crossing of the ways, not unlike, on an infinitesimal scale, the outburst of poetic genius at the end of the sixteenth century when commercial England had already begun to crush feudal England. The Histories and Tragedies of Shakespeare record the death of the old régime, and Doctor Faustus gives up feudal power for world power.[2]

Tate's comprehension of the meaning of the novel in his classic essay is primary—as the poetic drama was the form inherent in the Elizabethan literary subject, the novel is the form demanded by the subject of twentieth-century literature. The subject in the instances both of Elizabethan England and the modern American South is the same: the intense historical consciousness peculiar to an age which is at "a crossing of the ways." In such a period of endings and beginnings, the sense of time is heightened and a writer's consciousness struggles not only with the number of changes that are occurring, but, and

---

[2] Allen Tate, "The Profession of Letters in the South," in *Essays of Four Decades* (Chicago: Swallow Press, 1968), 533–34.

more profoundly, with their implications for his vision of human existence. The writer is acutely aware of life as it has been known, and will no longer be known. In the Elizabethan age the response of the literary imagination to the crisis in the vision of existence was made in the plays of Marlowe and Shakespeare; in the South of the 1920s and 1930s the response, as Tate sees it, is being made by such novelists as Elizabeth Madox Roberts, Caroline Gordon, Thomas Wolfe, Andrew Lytle, and William Faulkner. But in his analogy between the Elizabethan literary situation and that, in his own world, Tate fails to make a clear discrimination between the modern novel and the Elizabethan poetic drama. The Elizabethan tragedies respond to the declining vision of a world in which human events, obedient to a transcending myth of fate or destiny, move toward a climactic resolution. The novel answers to the need for a form to express the vision of a new and strange world in which the epic and/or tragic vision of time is being displaced by the assumption of time in the image of the mechanical clock—by the strange feeling that history is not a series of actions but a time process, in Quentin Compson's image, "a minute clicking of little wheels." [3]

The need for the novel was first answered by Cervantes. *Don Quixote* not only anticipates the shift in the modern consciousness from the mythic and traditionalist to the historical rationale of existence, but also diagnoses the psychic consequence of this alteration: the comic and pathetic individuation which occurs when, dislodged from the society of myth and tradition—from the cosmic sacramentalism of Christendom—the person begins to acquire, as we say, a personality. The Knight of the Sad Countenance becomes a self and goes in search of an identity in history. The individual, as creature of historical time, as a historical self—this is a theme in all modern literature in whatever form it is cast. But in the novel it appears with a singular

---

[3]*The Sound and the Fury* (New York: Vintage Books), 94.

concentration and comprehensiveness. The juxtaposition of the society of myth and tradition and the scientific-historical society in the acute consciousness of the novelist assumes, as in, say, *Pamela, Tom Jones, Tristram Shandy,* and *Madame Bovary,* the proportions of a literary myth of modern history. The novelistic vision translates the continuous dialectical tension established by the pressure of the past upon the present into a story in which the society of myth and tradition haunts the society of science and history.

In American literature the myth of the past in the present waited for its expression upon the expanding historical signification of the American Revolution. Receiving its first tentative formulation in the hastily written but discerning novels of Charles Brockden Brown, it came into distinct American versions in James Fenimore Cooper's stories about Leatherstocking, Edgar Allan Poe's tales about Roderick Usher and Ligeia, Nathaniel Hawthorne's depictions of Hester Prynne and the Reverend Mr. Dimmesdale, and preeminently in Herman Melville's story of Ishmael, Ahab, and Moby-Dick. But, it may be noted, the stories of Poe, Hawthorne, and Melville were not written primarily in the light of the Revolution; they appeared in the foreboding light of an approaching civil war in the new nation. In the great and terrible illumination of this conflict, when it came, the true past of the American existence—its deep substance in the ancient terrors of European history—found out the present. The nation that, flaunting all the historical evidence certifying man's irresistible disposition to folly and evil, had based itself on the premise that man is a rational and beneficent being, had within seventy years of the establishment of the Great Experiment in human nature engaged in one of the bloodiest internecine conflicts in history.

Yet the post–Civil War American novelistic vision by no means focused in a pessimistic view of history. Henry James, believing the truth of American history still to lie in the dynamics of the great moral experiment, opposed the essential innocence of the self liberated from the past to the evil intrinsic in the self implicated in European experience. The other most substantial American novelist of the post–Civil War America, William Dean Howells, also supported the moral superiority of the American present. Both James and Howells, to be sure, felt that asserting the triumph of American innocence was their historical responsibility as American authors.

Among the determinate motives of American novelists none is more ironic, nor so fundamental and so rich in meaning, as the compulsion to regard the individual as being responsible for history. The logic of this imperative is inescapable; it is the American idea in essence. Operating with an intense historical consciousness of what they were doing, a band of British subjects, centered in a few such cosmopolitan men of letters as Benjamin Franklin, Thomas Jefferson, and John Adams, became the first people in the annals of man deliberately to subvert the assumption of the past as the necessary inheritance of the present. Having successfully culminated this treason against Church and State and against all the mythic, traditionalist, and ceremonial structures of the mother country, they invented a republic purged of these structures; and, whether they fully intended to or not, dedicated the new nation to the historical fulfillment of human equality. The first nation deliberately to dispossess the past became the first to be possessed by the concept of modern history as a progressive enhancement of the status of the person. The Americans therefore became the first people to experience the internalization of history in the self as their necessary mode of being. This meant that the American became the first individual to be haunted not by a mythic and traditionalist past but by history. So tight has been the conjunction of history and self in the American concept of personal being that the American has feared that to be dispossessed by history means the loss of personal identity. One of the most significant stories in American literature is about such an experience—the plain yet graphic parable by Edward Everett Hale entitled "The Man Without a Country."

But the more complex American writers have not easily assumed with Hale that the American literary subject is the incarnation of historical responsibility in the individual. In a sense they have resisted this assumption because accepting it implies a deprivation for the American writer; for if his true subject is the resolution of the crossing of the ways in the American self, he does not share in the subject known to the general literary culture of the West—the myth of the past in the present. In a deeper sense American writers have drawn back from an unqualified embracement of the identity of the self and American history because it intimates more than a limitation of subject. It implies an end to the dialectic arising from the crossing of the ways, thereby suggesting not only a termination of the cultural dialectic arising from the crossing of the ways but the displacement of the whole modern literary culture, and possibly of the whole of Western letters. This intimation of the meaning of American historicism has been harbored in the American literary mind as a kind of secret knowledge. Its unspoken presence is evident in literary nationalists like Emerson and Whitman as well as in cosmopolitan conservatives like James and Eliot. One of its overt, or almost overt, manifestations occurs in Mark Twain, who, while not strictly speaking a southern writer, has vivid affinities with the South. I refer to his ironic inversion of the drama of the past in the present in *A Connecticut Yankee in King Arthur's Court*. As a prophetic work this novel transcends the mythic connection between past and present and assumes the quality of a world historical vision. The figure of Hank Morgan is a minor literary creation; but Hank, the morally ignorant but inventive Yankee who takes on the responsibility for the history of the Middle Ages in the name of the American doctrine of progress and in doing so destroys a world, is significant enough to stand beside Don Quixote. While the Knight of the Sad Countenance poignantly embodies the crossing of the ways, Hank decisively embodies its appalling resolution.

Twentieth-century southern writers, however close to James in sensibility, resemble Mark Twain in their apprehension of the power of modern history to resolve the modern literary dialectic. Their perception is not altogether owing to the South's heritage of defeat. The catastrophe of the Civil War confirmed intimations of historical displacement which had preyed upon southerners from the early days of the Virginia settlement. Like the adventitious rise of tobacco smoking in Europe, to which it was inextricably linked, chattel slavery was no part of Anglo-Saxon myth and tradition. On the contrary, the drastic effect of its casual introduction into the American South represents the radical power of modern history once it began to center in a world marketplace. Southerners understood that slavery was a historical accident and called it their "peculiar institution"; but, history demanding that they justify it as part of their civilizational heritage, they came to look upon it as providential. In their defense of the peculiar institution southern men of letters (in the encompassing sense of the terms *letters* and *literature* still obtaining in the nineteenth century, both the defense of slavery and the abolitionist attack on it were literary) attempted to adapt the slavery system to the general literary subject in Western culture, the myth of the past in the present. They envisioned a modern slave society in which a free and egalitarian republic of white men was assimilated at once to a world marketplace economy and to a recovery of a patriarchal and traditionalist society. In seeking to project their vision, southern writers followed the ultimate imperative of the modern historicist ethos: they rewrote history to make it conform to historical necessity. They placed the southern literary mind, as Henry James perceived, under the interdiction of a "new criticism"—a

southern critique of history.[4] This in effect meant a drastic assimilation of both the southern writer and his subject matter to the
present emergency of the state. The southern literary imagination
was thus strangely bereft by the historical action through which it
sought to fulfill itself. In the southern literary consciousness of the
1840s and 1850s the dialectical tension of the past in the present
was increasingly resolved in an immitigable historicism. Until the
southern literary imagination should be opened to the subject of
the past in the present, the southern novelist had no subject,
even though it was implicit in a commitment to history that obsessed the southern self in its blood and bone.

A larger vision of southern history was slowly beginning to
open to the novelist in the South when the First World War
erupted. But this cataclysmic event forcibly directed his attention outward toward the meaning of world history, and in
doing so toward the meaning of the South in this context. The
Civil War and the South's defeat took on the character of
events symbolizing the southern participation in the whole
civilizational drama of the past in the present. The southern
situation became emblematic of the crossing of the ways in
Western civilization, and the southern literary artist could view
himself both as observer of and participant in the crisis. Mark
Twain had glimpses of the possibilities open to the novelist
who could grasp southern history both sympathetically and
ironically, bringing into focus the fate of a slave society that had
been both historical novelty and anachronism. Faulkner was to
see the southern situation in full and to capture the entire drama
of the South's representation of the past in the present.

In accomplishing this great task Faulkner made an imaginary
southern world of which he was, as he said, sole proprietor—a
county in northern Mississippi modeled on his home county of
Lafayette, with its county seat of Oxford. He called his creation

---

[4]Henry James, *The American Scene* (New York: Charles Scribner's Sons, 1946), 374.

Yoknapatawpha County and named its seat Jefferson. But in spite of the fact that his invention and peopling of Yoknapatawpha is a major achievement in twentieth-century literature, Faulkner did not uniformly maintain the proprietorship of his mythical county during the forty years he wrote about it. At about midpoint in his authorial career his imaginative grasp of it weakened. His lapsing hold on Yoknapatawpha may be partially attributed to burdensome personal circumstances. It may be traced more surely, I think, to literary circumstances.

The most obvious of these circumstances was a middle-aged artist's experience of a falling off from creativity. In his younger years Faulkner was a singularly intense writer, so much so that he undoubtedly went through periods of composition when he became oblivious either to publishers or readers. When he reached his forties the spells of absolute absorption in writing appear to have become infrequent. This decline of creative intensity troubled him all the second half of his career. He softened it by saying that he had become more like Flaubert—no longer banging it on like an apprentice paperhanger, but, his skill honed by years of practicing his art, writing carefully and selectively, exercising the control of the master craftsman.[5] But such posing was histrionic self-irony. Germane to Faulkner's anxiety about his career was, we may conjecture from a perspective afforded by the later years of the twentieth century, a sense of crisis more profound than concern about a more or less normal attrition of artistic power. Like his contemporaries Eliot and Hemingway, Faulkner sensed an association between his experience of the crisis of middle age and the final falling off of literature from the fundamental modern subject. By the 1940s the literary history of the century clearly insinuated that while the First World War had heightened the dialectical play of the

---

[5]See Joseph Blotner, *Faulkner: A Biography* (New York: Random House, 1974), II, 1179.

crossing of the ways in the American (and modern) literary imagination, it had forecast the complete eclipse of the literary myth of modern history.

Such an awareness on Faulkner's part—his implied recognition of the disappearance of the past in the present as cultural theme and substance in the final historicizing of the mythic, ceremonial, sacramental world of Christendom—is a basic inhibitory influence on his largest non-Yoknapatawpha vision. This is the vision of Western civilization he struggled to set forth in *A Fable*. Begun in 1944, this novel occupied its author for ten years. A novel that may seem less compatible with Yoknapatawpha than any other of the non-Yoknapatawpha works—a piece that may seem to have intervened in and been detrimental to the development of Yoknapatawpha—*A Fable* bears an important relation to Faulkner's fictional dominion. Indeed it essentially affords a significant demarcation of first and second cycles of the Yoknapatawpha tales. In the first cycle, published between 1929 and 1942—*Sartoris, The Sound and the Fury, As I Lay Dying, Sanctuary, Light in August, Absalom, Absalom!, The Hamlet,* and *Go Down, Moses*—Faulkner achieved a major representation of the dialectical drama of the crossing of the ways. He performed the task, he said, in the sweat and agony of the spirit; yet, as he also said, in joy and, in a few moments, in ecstasy. The novels of the second cycle, published between 1948 and 1962—*Intruder in the Dust, Requiem for a Nun, The Town, The Mansion,* and *The Reivers*—written with labor but evidently less of joy and never in ecstasy—are a record of the decline of the civilizational or cultural rationale of the Yoknapatawphian subject.

A Fable, it may be said, is nothing less than an attempt to confront this decline and to arrest it. It is an effort to assert the fundamental rationale of Faulkner's vision of Yoknapatawpha, that is, its service as a microcosmic image of the literary myth of modern history.

This is not to say that in the first cycle of Yoknapatawpha

stories Faulkner comprehends the dialectical play of past and present in balanced tension. His attitude toward his subject is conditioned from the beginning by his sensitivity to its impermanence. In the pre–Yoknapatawpha publications—the poetic sequence called *The Marble Faun* and the novels *Soldiers' Pay* and *Mosquitoes*—Faulkner implies his awareness of the depletion of the Western mythic constructs and of the threatened loss of the myth-making capacity of the imagination. He invigorates, complicates, and expands the implication of poetic dispossession in the initial cycle of Yoknapatawpha works, transforming the life of the little patch of world that he staked out as his own into a drama of the subversion, or betrayal, of the older order of myth and tradition by the southern commitment to modern history. Exploring the character of Quentin Compson III—a character with whom he was fully empathetic and who is closer to being a fictive representation of the author than any other character in his stories—Faulkner developed a powerful symbol of the traumatic interiorization of modern history in the self. Quentin's strivings to transcend his feeling of guilt for the lapse of his family into disorder and decay lead him to imagine a myth of supreme damnation: he commits incest with his sister Caddy and the two are consigned forever to hell. But Quentin's desire for a supratemporal reference for his agony avails nothing against the historicism of his consciousness. In *Sanctuary* Faulkner's disposition to a historicist outlook would seem virtually to prevail. Temple Drake sitting at the last with her father in the Luxembourg Gardens—sullen, discontented, spiritually dead, while the music of Massenet dies in the descending twilight—is a symbol of the historical triumph of the waste land. Still, as the music and the whole scene in the garden of the dead queens suggests, the tension between the mythic and historical forces underlying the novel is vividly present. In *Light in August* Faulkner creates a more explicit tension between myth and history by presenting a tangled situation in which he contrasts

132

the Protestant anguish over history and sexuality and (as Faulkner described it in an interview) "a luminosity older than our Christian civilization." Coming "from back in the old classic times" of "fauns, satyrs, and the gods," this illumination, a light from Olympus suggested by the quality of light in a Mississippi August, is, Faulkner said, what the title of the novel refers to. In *Light in August* the story of Lena Grove is set against that of Joe Christmas and Joanna Burden. Modernity can never betray Lena. She walks, Faulkner states, in the light of "that pagan quality of being able to assume everything." Unashamed of the desire for her child, Lena follows convention and tries to find the child's father. "But as far as she was concerned, she didn't especially need any father for it, any more than the women that—on whom Jupiter begot children were anxious for a home and a father." Lena lives in the "luminous lambent quality of an older light than ours." [6] On the other hand, while Lena has her identity in the survival of cosmic being in man's consciousness, Joe Christmas and Joanna Burden are creatures of history and are doomed by its imperious necessities. In their lives, and in the life of the Reverend Gail Hightower, Faulkner perceives the chief source of the modern historicist ethos as Protestant Christianity. Answerable for the meaning of their lives, Joe, Joanna, and Hightower remind us of how complex the American burden of history becomes when the Jeffersonian and Protestant convictions of the self's obligation to history are joined; and they further remind us that such a union has characterized the southern vision of the self.

The contention of the mythic-traditionalist and the historical modes of being is more expansively dramatized and investigated in *Go Down, Moses*. The sections in this novel called "The Bear" and "Delta Autumn" tell about Isaac McCaslin's rejection of his

---

[6]Frederick L. Gwynn and Joseph L. Blotner (eds.), *Faulkner in the University* (New York: Vintage Books, 1965), 199.

heritage because of the curse of slavery. In his act of renunciation Ike declares himself answerable for history, yet his subsequent attempt to imitate the life of Christ is equivocal and probably, though he does not realize it, a way of evading a responsible self-existence. Insofar as Ike illustrates the endeavor of an educated, sensitive person to return to the mythic-traditionalist mode of being, he demonstrates the impossibility of the attempt. There can be no return from the self-consciousness of history to the mythic existence, not even for one who as a boy has been privileged to enter at least into the margins of the mythic. To live in the Olympian light is possible only for an atavistic creature like Lena.

The character in the first cycle of Yoknapatawpha tales who appears to come closest to a convincing transcendence of the modern bondage to historical consciousness is Dilsey in *The Sound and the Fury*. According to Faulkner's metaphysic of endurance as exemplified in Dilsey, the survival of the mythic consciousness and the imperatives of the historical consciousness unite in the unending drama of the human heart in conflict with itself. In this drama Faulkner seeks a myth of modern man. This myth would center, not in the struggle of man to achieve historical selfhood, but in his universal capacity to endure his own nature as man, in enduring this to realize his goodness and his evil, and in this realization to prevail over his confinement in historical circumstance. Nonetheless, considered as a whole, the first Yoknapatawpha cycle does not pursue the quest for a compelling, transcending myth of man with assurance. Faulkner's vision of his subject, the past in the present as evinced in the American South, is oriented toward a deprivation of a mythic-traditionalist past by a materialistic present and always inclines toward history as the controlling center of existence.

Obedient to the dialectical shape of his subject, however, Faulkner refused to seal his image of Yoknapatawpha in historical determinism. When the Second World War broke out, his sense of resistance to history was accentuated. After the war is won, he wrote to his stepson Malcolm Franklin in 1943, "then we must, we must clean the world's house so that man can live in it in peace again." Meanwhile Faulkner had begun work on a project which originated in an idea a Hollywood producer had for a movie script about the First World War. The idea involved a dramatization making use of legendary questions about the identity of the Unknown Solider buried under the Arch of Triumph. Combining the story of a mutiny of French troops on the Western Front with the notion that the Unknown Soldier is Christ, Faulkner eventually began to write a long story or novella and finally a full-length novel about the First World War. In late 1944, when he was still thinking about a story of around fifteen thousand words, he explained his conception to Robert Haas of Random House as follows: "The argument is (in the fable) in the middle of that war, Christ (some movement in mankind which wished to stop war forever) reappeared and was crucified again. We are repeating, we are in the midst of war again. Suppose Christ gives us one more chance, will we crucify him again, perhaps for the last time." Faulkner added that he did not intend "to preach at all." He summed up his argument: "We did this in 1918; in 1944 it not only MUST NOT happen again, it SHALL NOT HAPPEN again, i.e. ARE WE GOING TO LET IT HAPPEN AGAIN? now that we are in another war, where the third and final chance might be offered to save him." [7] He was putting his story "crudely" he told Haas; but it is clear that by this point Faulkner had discovered in his First World War story a challenge to explore his thought and emotion about the nature of man through a deep inquiry into the moral structure of Western civilization. As the inquiry became more elaborate and more intricate, it assumed the form of a massive, stylized, phil-

---

[7]Blotner, *Faulkner*, II, 1154.

osophical and allegorical fable about the nature of modern existence. Moving beyond the boundaries of Yoknapatawpha, Faulkner committed himself to the broadest possible frame of novelistic reference in his search for a myth of man.

Faulkner's undertaking was bolder than, if not as successful as, Milton's attempt to write the epic of the fall of man. Milton had a story to tell which embodied for him the truth of faith: he believed the poet could justify the ways of God to man. Faulkner, having no received truth of faith, sought to justify the ways of man to man by a mythic construction of his own devising. He envisioned the justification as being the intervention in history of the son of man, bringing the message that man has the capacity to spiritualize his own history. Utilizing a radical adaptation of the central part of the Christian myth, the events of the Passion Week, Faulkner intends in *A Fable* to transfer the Christian myth into the realm of a mystical humanism, which in his writings had developed as an uncertain foil to the ruthless historicism of modernity. To this end *A Fable* presents two exemplary fables. One is the tall tale, drawn from the realm of southern comedy, about the horse thieves, the British sentry and the Reverend Tobe Sutterfield, and the marvelous three-legged racing horse. The other is the story, derived from religious myth, of the corporal and his father (the supreme general of the Allied forces), about the mutiny led by the corporal, and the subsequent events of the "Passion Week." Apposite to each other, the fabulous tales become mingled in the novel. Faulkner obviously intends to accomplish the transfer of the Christian myth into secular terms—into a fable illustrating man's imaginative power to transform his history into transcendent myth—through its association with the story of the incredible horse. In this tale a deputy in pursuit of the thieves thinks the fugitives are as good as captured when a large reward is put up for their apprehension and the return of the horse. The "sum, the amount of the reward—the black, succinct evocation of that golden dream" on the poster—insures their fate, for a "simple turn of a tongue" will bring someone "that shining and incredible heap of dollars." The thieves are "doomed not at all because passion is ephemeral (which was why they had never found any better name for it, which was why Eve and the Snake and Mary and the Lamb and Ahab and the Whale and Androcles and Balzac's African deserter, and all the celestial zoology of horse and goat and swan and bull, were the firmament of man's history instead of the mere rubble of his past), nor even because the rape was theft and theft is wrong and wrong shall not prevail, but simply because, due to the sheer repetition of zeros behind a dollar-mark on a printed placard, everyone within eyerange or tonguespread . . . would be almost frantically attuned to the merest whisper regarding the horse's whereabouts." A story of unnamable desires and dreams is translated into folklore and myth; and the tale of the groom, the Negro preacher, and the stolen horse, far from becoming the "mere rubble of the past, the detritus of the historical record," has become a part of the living "firmament of man's history." [8]

But A Fable strangely fails in its larger purpose: to place the story of the corporal in the firmament of man's history. The fundamental reason for this, I think, is revealed in an exchange with a student at the University of Virginia in 1957:

Q. Can you make any comment on the part that the Old General plays in A Fable, who seemed to me to take two distinct, different parts if not more, in the theme of Passion Week, including the Three Temptations? Would you care to elaborate at all on that character?

A. Well, to me he was the dark, splendid, fallen angel. The good shining cherubim to me are not very interesting, it's the dark, gallant, fallen one that is moving to me. He was an implement, really. What I was writing about was the trilogy of man's conscience represented by the young British Pilot Officer, the Runner, and the Quartermaster

---

[8] A Fable (New York: The Modern Library, 1966), 160–61.

General. The one that said, This is dreadful, terrible, and I won't face it even at the cost of my life—that was the British aviator. The Old General who said, This is terrible but we can bear it. The third one, the battalion Runner who said, This is dreadful, I won't stand it, I'll do something about it. The Old General was Satan, who had been cast out of heaven, and—because God himself feared him.

Q. Well, what—the thing that puzzled me was that, going back, as far as I could gather, he also had been the father of the Corporal.

A. Yes, that's right.

Q. And that is what has somewhat puzzled me in the allegorical—

A. That was part of Satan's fearsomeness, that he could usurp the legend of God. That was what made him so fearsome and so powerful, that he could usurp the legend of God and then discard God. That's why God feared him.[9]

The student's hesitant and fumbling little inquisition broke off, but he had made a vital point. The Christ who is crucified in *A Fable* is conceived by Faulkner to be the son of man because he is the son of Satan, the rebel against God. At the funeral of the old general before "the vast and serene and triumphal and enduring Arch," the protest against militarism by the the corporal's disciple, the runner, hardly persuades us that the part of man's conscience which says "I'll do something about it" actually can do or wants to do anything about it.[10] In the "trinity of man's conscience" the voice of the runner is subordinate to that of the old general saying "This is terrible but we can bear it." It is the old general—Satan himself—and not the runner (in spite of Faulkner's attempt to make the disciple of the corporal the hero) who personifies the attributes of man most celebrated by Faulkner: the strength to endure his fate as the creature of his own history, and pride in the strength. The most eloquent and persuasive rhetoric in *A Fable* is the old general's. It is his (Satan's) apology for man that, in the temptation scene, strikes the truest note in the novel.

---

[9]Gwynn and Blotner (eds.), *Faulkner in the University*, 62–63.
[10]For the funeral scene, see *A Fable*, 433–37.

Then he said, "Afraid? No no, it's not I but you who are afraid of man;
not I but you who believe that nothing but a death can save him. I
know better. I know that he has that in him which will enable him to
outlast even his wars; that in him more durable than all his vices, even
that last and most fearsome one; to outlast even this next avatar of his
servitude which he now faces: his enslavement to the demonic progeny
of his own mechanical curiosity, from which he will emancipate himself
by that one ancient tried-and-true method by which slaves have always
freed themselves: by inculcating their masters with the slaves' own
vices—in this case the vice of war and that other one which is no vice at
all but instead is the quality-mark and warrant of man's immortality: his
deathless folly. . . . It will be his own frankenstein which roasts him
alive with heat, asphyxiates him with speed, wrenches loose his
still-living entrails in the ferocity of its prey-seeking stoop. So he will
not be able to go along with it at all, though for a little while longer it
will permit him the harmless delusion that he controls it from the
ground with buttons. Then that will be gone too; years, decades then
centuries will have elapsed since it last answered his voice; he will have
even forgotten the very location of its breeding-grounds and his last
contact with it will be a day when he will crawl shivering out of his
cooling burrow to crouch among the delicate stalks of his dead
antennae like a fairy geometry, beneath a clangorous rain of dials and
meters and switches and bloodless fragments of metal epidermis, to
watch the final two of them engaged in the last gigantic wrestling
against the final and dying sky robbed even of darkness and filled with
the inflectionless uproar of the two mechanical voices bellowing at each
other polysyllabic and verbless patriotic nonsense. O yes, he will
survive it because he has that in him which will endure even beyond
the ultimate worthless tideless rock freezing slowly in the last red and
heatless sunset, because already the next star in the blue immensity of
space will be already clamorous with the uproar of his debarkation, his
puny and inexhaustible voice still talking, still planning; and there too
after the last ding dong of doom has rung and died there will still be
one sound more: his voice planning still to build something higher and
faster and louder; more efficient and louder and faster than ever
before, yet it inherent with the same old primordial fault since it too in
the end will fail to eradicate him from the earth. I dont fear man. I do
better: I respect and admire him. And pride: I am ten times prouder of
that immortality which he does possess than ever he of that heavenly
one of his delusion. Because man and his folly—"

139

"Will endure," the corporal said.

"They will do more," the old general said proudly. "They will prevail." [11]

The supreme general knows what will happen in history. Moreover, he not only knows the futility of the myth of sacrifice the corporal is once again bequeathing to man, he knows that his son knows its futility. As the old general parts from his son, the corporal says, "Good-bye, Father." The father replies, "Not good-bye . . . . I am durable too; I dont give up easily either. Remember whose blood it is that you defy me with." [12] The corporal does indeed know his own blood. Both he and the dark angel who fathered him know that another futile sacrifice of it is necessary as a symbolic reaffirmation of the continuity of history in its essential meaning, the drama of man and his folly. This drama endures the rejection of even the noblest sacrifice; it never transcends itself. Insofar as man prevails, he prevails in the endurance of his history and not over it. This, I would suggest, is the underlying sense of one of the most powerful yet enigmatic scenes in A Fable. I speak of the one when the French army chaplain comes to the corporal with his priestly "gear"— "urn ewer stole candles and crucifix"—to adminster the Last Sacraments.[13] But first he must follow an order from the old general to make a final plea to the corporal to reconsider his commitment to martyrdom. In the course of his discussion with the corporal, the priest realizes that he has lost a Christ whose presence is invoked in the transcendent mystery of the mass, the Christ of the institutional Church (the Lamb of God who takes away the sins of the world) and found in the illiterate corporal a Christ who appears as the human spirit in human history (as Faulkner said in his letter to Robert Haas, "some movement in

---

[11]Ibid., 352–54.
[12]Ibid., 356.
[13]Ibid., 367.

mankind which wished to stop war forever"). To atone, it would seem, for his, or the Church's, delusion about the nature of the human spirit—the failure to recognize the true meaning of the crucifixion as an act affirming man's nature—the priest runs a bayonet into his side. He repeats the ritualistic thrust of the spear by the Roman soldier into the body of Christ at Golgotha, in this gesture identifying himself with the Christ who is the creature of history and with the corporal, who is the son of the proud angel who fell into human history.

Although *A Fable* refers often to the ironic dualities which mark human existence, the novel culminates in no vision of mundane history differentiated from a transcending firmament of history. In fact, although the question of whether or not Satan has verily usurped the legend of God is raised solely as poetic possibility in *A Fable*, the identification of the dramatic, story telling,–the literary–imagination with the "dark, splendid, fallen angel" is unmistakable. (Faulkner's depiction of the educated and matchless parable-maker, the Christ of the New Testament, as an illiterate is part of the strategy of the novel.) If there is any doubt about the identification of Satan as world historical poet, it is removed when we compare the rhetoric of the old general with that of the famous Nobel Prize address. In *A Fable* Faulkner not only accepts a fall of modern man from the mythic into the historical mode of existence but concludes that the modern literary imagination cannot reverse this fall. Man's immortality is the unending succession of mortal lives in human history. History is the idiom of being.

The stories of the second Yoknapatawpha cycle confirm the unstated conclusion of *A Fable*. In them the association of a myth of man with the crossing of the ways—with the dialectic involving a mythic-traditionalist past and a historical present— gives way to the conception that the myth of man consists in his fall into a historical condition which is unredeemable save in his struggle to redeem it.

141

We note how in *Intruder in the Dust* Chick Mallison finally refers his participation in the history of Jefferson to the stasis of the actor's role. The actor has some control in the interpretation of the part he plays, but in any event he plays the role to its assigned conclusion. What Chick learns—I do not mean to say overtly—is that the community of man is the drama of history. Each person plays his role in the drama, but the mythic firmament, the supporting ground of transcendent meaning, is no firmer than Gavin Stevens's rhetoric. It is just that—rhetoric. The opposition of historical actuality and mythic transcendence in *Intruder in the Dust* is a static not an evolving drama.

This is true too of *Requiem for a Nun*. Faulkner invents a redemptionary scheme not unlike that in *A Fable*; but it is more bizarre in its effect, for it is accommodated to a realistic rather than to a fabulous story. Condemned to hang for murdering Temple's baby, an act she has committed in order to save Temple from herself, Nancy can hardly be taken as a symbol of a secularized Christ legend. The story about Temple and Nancy describes Nancy as a nun and the bride of Christ, not as the daughter of man, and so projects the Christian story as, conceivably, historical reality. Brought into juxtaposition with Faulkner's assimilation of history and myth in the progressive unfolding of the story of Jefferson in the eloquent prologues to the three acts of the novel-play, Nancy's literalistic acceptance of the necessity of sin, suffering, faith, and redemption contrasts vividly yet subtly with the transference of history into the mythic imagination—so "vast, so limitless" in its power to "disperse and burn away the rubble-dross of fact and probability, leaving only truth and dream." [14] Nancy's violent act of murdering the baby and her own imminent death by execution recall the grim blood sacrifices recorded in the Bible, each an act performed in the name of a divinely decreed historical scheme.

---

[14]*Requiem for a Nun* (New York: Random House), 226.

To escape her suffering, Temple tries to conceive of herself as existing only in the present. She is Mrs. Gowan Stevens; Temple Drake is dead with a dead past. Prompted by the moral tutelage of Gavin Stevens and Nancy, Temple responds to Gavin's dictum: "The past is never dead. It's not even past." [15] Accepting the truth of history, she comes to life as a living soul. But whether the soul can have a resting place without a full faith in a literal heaven transcending empirical history thereupon becomes Temple's anguished question. Resisting Nancy's simple admonition, "Believe," Temple reflects the Shakespearean mood Faulkner had drawn upon twenty years earlier in *The Sound and the Fury.* "What about me?" she asks. "Even if there is one [a heaven] and somebody waiting in it to forgive me, there's still tomorrow and tomorrow. And suppose tomorrow and tomorrow and then nobody there, nobody waiting to forgive me—" [16]

The last two novels of the Snopes trilogy, *The Town* and *The Mansion,* make explicit a theme Faulkner implies in *A Fable, Intruder in the Dust,* and Requiem for a Nun; history is the pathetic deprivation of the mythic existence. Actually this theme is anticipated in the first Snopes novel, *The Hamlet.* In this story Flem and Eula are up to their ears in conventional existence but bear always the signs of their beginnings in Faulkner's fascination with satyrs and fauns, demons and goddesses. Doomed by their presence in history but undoomed by the conflicts of the human heart, they exist in a curiously ambivalent connection to the historical motives that provide the context of their lives. Faulkner strives in *The Town* to make them vulnerable to the force of warring human passions. But he is uncertain of their strengths and fallibilities. He makes them convincing neither as displaced creatures of myth nor as

---

[15] *Ibid.,* 92.
[16] *Ibid.,* 283.

creatures of a historical society. Eula kills herself in *The Town*. Ostensibly she is obedient to social convention, wanting to save her daughter, Linda, from the knowledge that Flem is not her father. But, as Ratliff discerns, she kills herself to escape the town's efforts to reduce her to human status. A goddess displaced in history has had enough of it. In *The Mansion*, the last volume of the Snopes trilogy, Flem also has had enough. He sits in his lonely mansion as though waiting for his brother Mink to come and kill him. When Mink shows up with a rusty pistol that misfires and has to be recocked, Flem makes no gesture to save himself.

Faulkner remarks in a prefatory note to *The Mansion* that between the initial conception of the Snopes story in 1925 and its completion in 1959 he had "learned . . . more about the human heart and its dilemmas." [17] What he had learned generally speaking was mostly a confirmation of what he knew to begin with—namely, that the myths that represent the human heart in its complex desires and conflicts belong not to a realm which transcends human history but to the heart's impossible longing for transcendence. But the diminution of the dialectical drama of the past in the present in Faulkner's imagination eventuated in a tendency for Faulkner (like the later Mark Twain) to envision history as morally nihilistic yet eloquently pathetic. In *The Mansion* the interwoven stories of Flem and Eula, Gavin Stevens, V. K. Ratliff, Linda Snopes, and the others arrive at the simple, bleak summation of all human motives pronounced by Stevens and Ratliff:

> "There aren't any morals," Stevens said.
> "The pore sons of bitches," Ratliff said.
> "The poor sons of bitches," Stevens said. [18]

---

[17] *The Mansion* (New York: Vintage Books, 1959), ix.
[18] *Ibid.*, 429.

This austere resolution of the literary myth of modern history—of the moral drama of the past in the present as the subject of the literary imagination—is mitigated by Mink's compelling perception of his ultimate fate, as this is interpreted by the omniscient narrator of the last chapter of *The Mansion*. Mink, lying down on the earth, feels himself "following all the little grass blades and tiny roots, the little holes the worms made, down and down into the ground already full of the folks that had the trouble but were free now . . . all mixed up and jumbled up comfortable . . . equal to any, good as any, brave as any, being inextricable from, anonymous with all of them: the beautiful, the splendid, the proud and the brave, right on up to the very top itself among the shining phantoms and dreams which are the milestones of the long human recording—Helen and the bishops, the kings and the unhomed angels, the scornful and graceless seraphim." [19]

The signs in the firmament of myth are assimilated into the long human recording; the mythic consciousness becomes a part of the pathos of human history. It is to be expected that Faulkner's last novel, *The Reivers: A Reminiscence*, displays merely the vestiges of the great drama of myth and history which runs through the Yoknapatawpha saga. Lucius Priest, the eleven-year-old boy who is the teller of the story, is to some extent an autobiographical persona. Although the story he relates has sharply realistic elements, Lucius concludes the monumental series of stories with an affectionate, nostalgic celebration of the events in his life in the year 1905. The civilizational tension of the crossing of the ways quietly vanishes in a past that has no present.

---

[19]*Ibid.*, 435–36.

Faulkner's Universality

CALVIN S. BROWN

Earlier I stood here and pointed out in some detail how
thoroughly and minutely Faulkner's most important work is, like
a medieval serf, bound to the soil of his own county and its
fictional counterpart. Now I have the effrontery to appear before
you again to maintain that his best work is essentially universal.
A decent respect to the opinions of mankind (as the Declaration
of Independence phrases it) would seem to demand some sort of
explanation.

The first thing to be cleared up is that this discussion is no
palinode or recantation. It in no way denies anything that I said
before. In fact, it does not modify my earlier statement in any
particular. What it does attempt to do is to expand it and add to
it some highly significant facts that are necessarily missed in any
discussion limited to Faulkner's localism.

When we speak of universality in a work of art, we have a
generally but somewhat vaguely understood idea in mind.
Obviously, we do not mean that every single human being in the
world finds the work interesting, or relevant to himself, or even
comprehensible. But we do mean that its appeal is not confined
within any narrow limits of space or time. Spatially, universality
requires that a work be able to grip people of different nations,
latitudes, and hemispheres; that it be capable of overleaping the
mental barriers not merely between Baptists and Methodists, or
Catholics and Protestants, but those that separate Christians,

Jews, Mohammedans, Hindus, and Buddhists; that it recognize no bounds of social or economic classes—in short, that, like Joy in Schiller's ode, it make all human beings become brothers under its wing. Or perhaps, in the light of current emphases, I should revise Schiller to make him say that all persons become siblings.

In time, we demand—or, in the case of contemporaries, rashly predict—the same sort of extension. A work so dated as to be merely topical may have an ephemeral worldwide vogue, but it has no universality and hence no staying power. In the context of universality, a work may appeal strongly to several generations and still be ephemeral—like Owen Meredith's poem *Lucile,* which was published in England in 1860, went through more than ninety editions in the United States alone, and is now probably the most secondhand book in existence. If *Lucile* has a long life in comparison with a subliterary phenomenon like *Roots,* it is itself clearly ephemeral when set beside the work of Homer, Vergil, Dante, Cervantes, Molière, Goethe, or any number of other writers whom we can call truly universal. Nevertheless, there is probably a limit to the temporal endurance of any literary work. Eventually, it would seem, problems of language, changes in human attitudes, and totally different ways of life may reduce any literary work from a real presence to an antiquarian curiosity. Homer's power seems undiluted even today, but the Babylonian epic of *Gilgamesh* cannot speak to us in the same way, interesting though it may be. We can still become one with Homer, but we cannot really enter into *Gilgamesh,* or it into us.

When I call Faulkner universal, then, I am predicting for him the power of endurance of the great literary classics. This is, I realize, a rash and possibly a brash judgment, but it is safe enough as a practical matter because if I am wrong we will never know it. I can at least be confident that Faulkner's work will outlast all of us.

Faulkner's Universality

One sign of Faulkner's standing is his reception abroad. In fact, he was really taken seriously in France before he was in his own country. When Malcolm Cowley first began to plan the Viking *Portable Faulkner* in 1945, Faulkner was still regarded in this country as an eccentric regional writer, but Cowley was able to tell him that Jean Paul Sartre had said, "Pour les jeunes en France, Faulkner c'est un dieu." [1] It is obvious that the young intellectuals in France at this time knew little and cared less about the South, the Civil War, our racial dilemmas, honeysuckle romance, hookworm realism, or any of the other immediate aspects of Faulkner's work that loomed so large in the minds of his American critics. They were simply protected by their own ignorance from much concern with these matters. Since Faulkner's localism meant nothing to them, it could not obscure the view of his universality. The same thing is true all over the world. Faulkner has something profound to say to many peoples who are even less attuned to our regional concerns and folkways than were the young French intellectuals of 1945.

We are confronted, then, with the essential question: how can a writer as intensely local as Faulkner be, at the same time, truly universal?

Most scholars who have glanced at this problem have given one of two answers, or a combination of the two. They have said that Faulkner somehow became universal by drawing on the works of past writers who had this quality. Or they have said that he achieved this feat by working into his novels the great myths which speak to the concerns of all mankind. Or they have said both these things. There is some truth in both, of course, but a good deal more error.

Before we can really look into this question, however, we must make a little excursion which may look like a digression, but actually is not. Faulkner's critics are very largely academics,

---

[1] Joseph Blotner, *Faulkner: A Biography* (New York: Random House, 1974), 1187.

and they, like most people, have a very high regard for themselves. (Having been one practically all my life, I can speak with some authority.) The academic mind admires itself and consequently tends to assume that admirable people must be scholars. And since the academics admire Faulkner, it follows that he must be a scholar. This is an underlying (and false) assumption in a great deal of Faulkner criticism.

Faulkner himself never tired of stating the contrary, but his own witness has been largely disregarded, and with some justice. For various reasons which were probably not too clear to himself, he made all sorts of false or wildly exaggerated statements about himself, like his repeated assertions that he was a combat flier in France in World War I—actually, he was still in ground school in Canada when the war ended—and that he was a professional rum-runner on the Gulf Coast during Prohibition. A similar pose was that he was not really a writer, but just a Mississippi farmer who liked to spin yarns on paper. In the same way, Byron never dropped the affectation of being, not a poet, but merely a British lord who amused himself from time to time by scribbling verses. And in this same vein, Faulkner repeatedly insisted that he wasn't interested in ideas, but in people, and that he wasn't concerned with symbols and myths, but was simply trying to tell his story as best he could.

All these things must be considerably discounted, but they cannot be entirely dismissed. Faulkner was certainly a serious and dedicated artist, but he did not have the *theoretical* interest in technique of a Mallarmé or a Henry James, nor did he have their intense self-consciousness about their own practices. I shall return later to his use of myths and of other literature, but first something must be said about his reading.

The basic fact is that, as far as literature was concerned, he was almost entirely self-taught. Phil Stone gave him some directions and suggested some things that he read, but he moved out from under this tutelage considerably sooner than

Phil was willing to admit. The most striking thing about the learning of a self-taught person is how spotty and unpredictable it is. Such a person will display remarkable knowledge of recondite matters at one moment, and the next moment betray an astonishing ignorance of almost elementary things. When Faulkner published his early book of poems, A *Marble Faun*, my father asked him whether it was a good idea for an unknown writer to use a title which was already well known—and Faulkner asked in reply whether there was some other book with that name. Some academics have assumed that this was a deadpan joke, but it is actually very unlikely that at that time Faulkner knew or even knew of Hawthorne's novel. You cannot assume, without some good evidence, that Faulkner either had or had not read any particular author or work of literature.

Even less can you assume that his habit of mind and way of work were the academic ones of outline, research, and note-taking. Some excellent novelists, like Zola and Thomas Mann, have worked that way, but Faulkner did not. Yet many studies digging out minute, systematic, laborious parallels to earlier works make precisely this assumption. They assume that Faulkner was working in the manner of Joyce's *Ulysses*, though the possibility of Zola's *La Faute de l'Abbé Mouret*, written nearly half a century earlier and using the same "mythic" method, is at least as great. But Faulkner attempted this sort of thing only once, in *A Fable*, and it did not quite come off.

It may be worthwhile to look at a single instance of detailed scholarship wrongly attributed to Faulkner. Several critics have assumed that he had a detailed knowledge of Homer and used him extensively. He does like to talk about Helen of Troy. In fact, on one occasion, Ratliff reports that Gavin Stevens, talking about the great *femmes fatales* of heroic legend—Judith, Lilith, Francesca, Isolde—explained Helen's preeminence very simply: "It's because the others all talked. They are fading steadily into the obscurity of their own vocality within which their passions and tragedies took place. But not Helen. Do you know there is not one recorded word of hers anywhere in existence, other than that one presumable Yes she must have said that time to Paris?" [2] This sounds fine if you read it (as you are supposed to) trustingly, and pass on. But the simple fact is that thousands of words have been attributed to Helen. Even if we leave out latecomers like Giraudoux and Goethe, we can cite the fact that she is the principal character in, and gives her name to, one of the plays of Euripides, and has an important role in two others. But perhaps Euripides is too late too, and the passage refers to the real source, Homer himself. That won't work either. Helen appears in both the *Iliad* and the *Odyssey*, speaking a total of 114 lines—and Homeric hexameters are long lines. In the *Odyssey* she has one single speech 40 lines long, so that she is more nearly garrulous than silent.

Gavin Stevens is supposed to be a fine Greek scholar, and certainly this is not supposed to be his error. It is Faulkner's error, but only from an academic point of view. It sounds good in its context, and Faulkner neither knew nor cared whether or not it was true. Nor do I mean to criticize him—no one in his right mind would read *The Mansion* for classical scholarship. But the fact does emerge very clearly that Faulkner had nothing resembling the detailed familiarity with the Homeric poems that some pursuers of myths and sources have attributed to him.

There are, of course, such things as literary sources, and their study is a legitimate and interesting concern of scholarship. If the study is to mean anything, however, it must be pursued with some rigor of method and insistence on evidence that will stand up to examination. The best evidence is actual verbal similarities too close to be the result of coincidence. And the worst evidence—in fact, it is not evidence at all—is the occurrence of similar common narrative themes. I believe that it was Goethe

---

[2]*The Mansion*, 133.

(though I can't remember just where) who was accused of plagiarising Homer because he had one of his characters, admiring an admirable girl, comment that the man who won her would be a lucky man, and Odysseus had said the same thing about Nausikaa. With a simple common sense that often eludes the academic mind, Goethe commented that these were the natural sentiments of any normal man under the circumstances and that no writer would need to steal them from Homer or from anyone else.

Yet we continue to find this sort of approach. In *As I Lay Dying*, for example, we have a basic and ancient theme. But one critic assumes a bookish source. "This burial journey," he writes, "is found in many legends and tales since medieval times." (He might better have said since ancient Egyptian times.) "Though I have been unable to locate the particular one, I feel fairly sure that what the author has done has been to start with the basic story in one of these legends, transplant it to Frenchman's Bend, and then present it by modern subjective methods. How closely the author stuck to an original story we can never tell until the hypothetical original has been found." [3] A few years later, talking about the genesis of the same work, Faulkner told Jean Stein, "I simply imagined a group of people and subjected them to the simple universal natural catastrophes, which are flood and fire, with a simple natural motive to give direction to their progress." [4] The principle of Ockham's razor applies here: assume nothing more than you have to. Why— especially since there is no reason to think that Faulkner knew much medieval literature—hypothesize a recondite literary source for a journey beset with fire and flood, which are, as Faulkner says, "the simple universal natural catastrophes"? The key word, of course, is *universal*.

---

[3] Earl Miner, *The World of William Faulkner* (Durham: Duke University Press, 1952), 117.
[4] James B. Meriwether and Michael Millgate (eds.), *Lion in the Garden: Interviews with William Faulkner* (New York: Random House, 1968), 244.

No one denies that Faulkner was influenced by earlier writers. Balzac, Dostoevski, and Conrad are obvious examples. But he was not inclined to base his work on minute study and ingenious deliberate parallels, as some critics insist. To take the obvious example (always excepting *A Fable*), the title of *Absalom, Absalom!* points to the Old Testament parallel, but the novel certainly makes no attempt to work it out in detail. This fact can be most clearly seen by comparing Faulkner's novel with Dryden's satire, *Absalom and Achitophel*, where the correspondence between the biblical story and the characters and events which later led to Monmouth's rebellion in England are minutely elaborated.

The matter of myth has been, if possible, even more abused than that of literary sources. Faulkner had picked up, as any intelligent general reader must, a good general knowledge of the main classical myths as well as the obvious biblical ones. But it does not follow that he was a scholar in the field, like Sir James Frazer or Jessie Weston, nor that when he makes a casual passing allusion to Persephone or Atalanta we will find the complete myth exhaustively concealed, if only we look long and ingeniously enough.

Myth-hunting has become a compulsive sport recognizing neither closed seasons nor bag limits, and it is often pursued for its own sake, almost without reference to the work in which the hunt takes place. There is, for example, an article proving that Popeye, the Memphis gangster of *Sanctuary*, is really Hermes[5]—though it neglects to show why he *should* be Hermes, or what this identification contributes to an understanding of the novel. It does, however, point out a number of ways in which the character and activities of Popeye can be equated with those of Hermes.

I find this demonstration unconvincing, however, because

---

[5]Robert Slabey, "Faulkner's *Sanctuary*," *Explicator*, 22 (January, 1963), Item 45.

I know that Popeye is really Moses. The evidence is over-whelming. Popeye is a lawgiver to his group, as Moses is to the children of Israel. Moses, early in life, watered flocks; later, with his rod, he produced water in the desert for his people. This is all paralleled by the fact that Popeye with his rod (as an auto-matic is called in gangster slang) was a bootlegger providing drink for the thirsty populace of Memphis during Prohibition. The Lord forbids Moses any drinking before going to the taber-nacle, on pain of death; the doctors told Popeye that even a small amount of alcohol would kill him. Moses' rod becomes a serpent, as Popeye's automatic is a thing of evil. The rod also has obvious phallic symbolism, and just as Moses is shown the rod-serpent trick, but Aaron performs it, so Red performs the sexual act with Temple for the impotent Popeye. Aaron also speaks for Moses—remember that speaking is *intercourse*. In fact, Temple represents the bush which burned with fire and was not con-sumed. Moses was "slow of speech and of a slow tongue"; Popeye "did not learn to walk and talk until he was about four years old," and he was always laconic. Moses is given repeated instructions about cutting up sacrifices and killing two turtle-doves as an atonement for sin; as a child Popeye cut up two lovebirds—an obvious equivalent of turtledoves—and a kitten. Popeye took Temple Drake from the Old Frenchman Place to Miss Reba's, as Moses led the children of Israel out of the wilderness to the promised land. It may seem strange to equate a brothel with the promised land, but this is characteristically Faulknerian, as is shown by the first name of *Temple* Drake and by his calling Nancy Mannigoe a nun. This equation is proved by the fact that the brothel may be considered to be flowing with semen—a milky fluid—and Miss Reba regularly calls Temple Drake "Honey." The bizarre rape of Temple and her subsequent bleeding represent the dividing of the Red Sea. And, finally, the Lord tells Moses, "And these are they which ye shall have in abomination among the fowls: . . . the owl . . . and the little owl

. . . and the great owl." At the Old Frenchman Place, Popeye is irrationally terrified by a swooping owl. There are still other parallels between Moses and Popeye, but surely these are enough to prove the case beyond any reasonable doubt.[6]

I hope that no one suspects me of believing a word of this nonsense; I was simply trying to show how fatally easy and how absurd this sort of myth-mongering is. Given two fairly elaborate stories or biographies, one can, with a bit of ingenuity and forcing, find parallels and make them seem striking. Popeye as Moses looks pretty good—but I am confident that I could work out an equally convincing case for Genghis Khan or Joan of Arc—or, for that matter, for Goldilocks or Idi Amin.

The rejection of this sort of naïvely ingenious myth-hunting, however, does not mean that Faulkner's work has nothing to do with the great myths. Quite the contrary. What it does mean is that one does not achieve universality or literary immortality by parodying or merely alluding to tales which have already achieved these qualities. Such triviality has no place in either myth or literature. The connection is deeper and more serious.

In spite of all sorts of possible complications, a true myth has two essential characteristics. First, it is a story that somehow embodies basic human problems, attitudes, and beliefs. Historical truth is of no importance whatsoever here: it is moral truth that is required. Every people has its own creation myth which lives quite independently of the findings of astrophysics and geology. The second characteristic of a real myth is that it be a part of the thinking of a considerable group of more or less homogenous people. Notice that I do not say that it must be believed. I do not believe *Genesis*, but nevertheless it is my creation myth, and it lives in my mind, and that of millions of

---

[6]Since this whole identification of Popeye with Moses is a deliberate exercise in futility, it is hardly worthwhile to document it. I can assure the reader, however, that there is no cheating and that everything I have cited can be found in the Pentateuch or in *Sanctuary*.

other modern Occidentals, in a way that the Mayan and Polynesian accounts of creation do not.

Faulkner commented on this *presence* of myth, regardless of belief, when a student at the University of Virgina asked about his repeated use of crucifixion imagery. "Remember," Faulkner replied, "the writer must write out of his background. He must write out of what he knows . . . and that was a part of my background. I grew up with that. I assimilated that, took that in without even knowing it. It's just there. It has nothing to do with how much of it I might believe or disbelieve—it's just there." [7] It is worth noting that Goethe made a similar, though much more self-conscious, observation about his use of heaven, saints, and angelic choruses in the final scene of *Faust*. "The end, with the ascending soul," he told his young friend Eckermann, "was very hard to write, and in dealing with such transcendental, almost inconceivable things I could easily have lost myself in vagueness if I had not given my poetic intentions a helpfully enclosed form and solidity by means of the sharply defined ecclesiastical Christian figures and concepts." [8]

Alongside the serious literary and historical use of the word *myth* to designate the basic narratives and perceptions of humanity, there is a recent journalistic use to mean merely a silly, untrue notion. It is in this sense that we hear people speak of the myth that fat people are happy, or that women are unintelligent. Many words have several meanings, of course, and no harm is done unless we confuse them. In Faulkner criticism, however, we do find a strange muddle in these two meanings. The very same critics who praise Faulkner for his incorporation of the great myths into his work are very often the ones who berate him for using what they call the myth (in the journalistic sense) of the antebellum South and the Civil War.

[7]Frederick L. Gwynn and Joseph L. Blotner (eds.), *Faulkner in the University: Class Conferences at the University of Virginia, 1957–1958* (New York: Vintage, 1965), 86.
[8]Goethe, *Gespräche mit Eckerman*, June 6, 1831 (my translation).

They deploy a good deal of historical apparatus to disprove this "myth," and seem to think that it can be dismissed out of hand in this way. What they do not realize (or at least refuse to admit) is that it is a real myth, and that strict historical accuracy applies to it no more and no less than to that other lost and scorched paradise, the Garden of Eden. The tacit assumption is that other nations are entitled to their myths, but the South is not.

There is an interesting example of this attitude in the attacks that have been made on a passage almost at the end of *Sartoris*. Commenting on the tradition and name of the Sartoris family, Faulkner says, "For there is death in the sound of it, and a glamorous fatality, like silver pennons downrushing at sunset, or a dying fall of horns along the road to Roncevaux." Critics routinely comment that this is sheer romantic nonsense, that you cannot legitimately compare a gang of harebrained swashbucklers like the Sartorises with Roland and Oliver and with a great poem like the *Song of Roland*—which the majority of Faulkner critics probably have not actually read. You can't compare the fake heroics of southern aristocracy with the real heroics of medieval France, they say.

But the argument boomerangs. In the *Chanson de Roland*, an epic battle in the pass of Roncevaux pitted Christians against pagans in a splendid show of loyalty, heroism, the true faith, and "sweet France" versus treachery, deceit, wicked idolatry, and the powers of darkness. But our best sober history tells that what actually happened on the afternoon of August 15, 778, was that Charlemagne's rearguard was cut to pieces in a pass of the Pyrenees, not by Saracens, but by a bunch of local Basque freebooters. In strict history, the deaths of Roland and Oliver were just about as heroic as that of Hightower's grandfather in *Light in August*. It would be reckless to assert that Faulkner knew this and intended its irony—though, considering the nature of his undisciplined reading, that is entirely possible. What we can see clearly enough, though, if we do not simply refuse to do so, is that the southern myth of the Civil War is no more to be denigrated by historical criticism than is the French myth of the *Song of Roland*. Both are viable and valuable myths with a substratum of genuine history and a superstructure of glamorous legend.

When Aristotle said that poetry is more philosophical than history, he was referring to the poetry in which the great Greek myths are incorporated. Nietzsche, in *The Birth of Tragedy*, is much more specific. "A people, like an individual," he wrote, "is worth something only to the extent to which it is able to put the stamp of eternity onto its own experiences, because by so doing it is freed from the world and at the same time shows its unconscious inner conviction of the relativity of time and of the true—that is, the metaphysical—significance of life. The opposite happens when a people begins to understand itself historically and to raze its metaphysical fortifications—a process which normally involves a decided worldlyfication, a break with the unconscious metaphysics of its earlier existence, with all its ethical consequences." [9]

The connection between great literature and a feeling for myth is clear enough, but it is all too often turned upside down. Certainly Faulkner had a general familiarity with the great myths and frequently referred to them or used them in passing, though I maintain that, except for *A Fable*, he did not found whole works on them in elaborate paraphrase, in the manner of Joyce's *Ulysses*. But he does not become universal by drawing on them. If universality could be so easily and mechanically obtained, all the colossal bulk of third- and fourth-rate poetry on themes drawn from classical mythology would be universal instead of utterly dead. Faulkner's universality does not arise from his parallels with the myths. The opposite is true: the parallels are due to his universality.

---

[9]Nietzsche, *Die Geburt der Tragödie aus dem Geiste der Musik*, Ch. 23 (my translation).

He himself understood this point and stated it clearly in a letter to Malcolm Cowley in the fall of 1944:

I'm inclined to think that my material, the South, is not very important to me. I just happen to know it, and don't have time in one life to learn another one and write at the same time. Though the one I know is probably as good as another, life is a phenomenon and not a novelty . . . . Art is simpler than people think because there is so little to write about. All the moving things are eternal in man's history and have been written before, and if a man writes hard enough, sincerely enough, humbly enough, and, with the unalterable determination never never never to be quite satisfied with it he will repeat them, because art like poverty takes care of its own.[10]

In other words, Faulkner did not need some undiscovered medieval tale of a journey to suggest that he subject the Bundrens to "the simple universal natural catastrophes, which are fire and flood." Faulkner's parallels to the myths are not the cause of his universality, but its result. We must look elsewhere for the cause.

It is obvious that the principal cause is a certain quality of mind, but this observation does not get us very far, since everything in a writer's work, good or bad, is obviously the result of the quality of his mind. The real question, then, is whether we can break down the quality of mind that might be called universal into any identifiable subheads, any recognizable habits, attitudes, or components of any sort. Such an attempt cannot, of course, ever be completely successful, nor can it be convincing to everyone, but still it seems at least worth trying. Something might come of it, even if it is not exactly what we were after when we started.

One of the simplest and clearest, though not the most im-

---

[10]Joseph Blotner (ed.), *Selected Letters of William Faulkner* (New York: Random House, 1977), 185–86.

portant, of the universal characteristics of Faulkner's mind is his
fondness for aphorisms. Though the fact has not been much
noted, he is a great aphorist. Both in his own person as narrator
and through the mouths of his characters, he is constantly
relating the particular case to generally prevailing, universal
statements like "The first principle of the law is, God alone
knows what the jury will do." Many of his aphorisms are, like
this one, humorous, but it is only a shallow mind that fails to see
that much humor is fundamentally a good deal more serious than
is a great deal of pompous effort to be philosophical. There is a
profound and compassionate view of the human condition, in all
lands and all ages, in the comment "Man aint really evil, he jest
aint got any sense." This observation is balanced by the
charitable conviction that "Most men are a little better than
their circumstances give them a chance to be." Ambrose Bierce
defined *positive* as "mistaken at the top of one's voice." The
same universal observation is concealed in the statement "Hit's
de folks dat says de high watter cant git dis fur dat comes floatin
out on de ridge-pole." In *The Reivers*, Ned abstracts the essential character of the unspeakable Otis from all purely local or
temporal ties with the remark "He the sort that no matter how
bad you think you need him, you find out afterward you was
better off." A few more examples (out of a great many) will drive
home the point of Faulkner's tendency to universalize by
aphorism. "Curiosity is another of the mistresses whose slaves
decline no sacrifice." "The past is never dead. It's not even
past." "What do you want with justice when you've already got
welfare?" "People are far more tolerant of artists than artists are
of people." "Ever' now and then a feller has to walk up and spit
in deestruction's face, sort of, fer his own good." [11]

Another characteristic of universality is its devotion to even-

---

[11]*Sanctuary*, 316–17; *The Mansion*, 230; *Go Down, Moses*, 345; *The Sound and the
Fury*, 133; *The Reivers*, 168; *The Mansion*, 343; *Requiem for a Nun*, 92; *The Mansion*,
207; *Mosquitoes*, 270; *Sartoris*, 205.

handed justice. The great works are never parochial or partisan. The *Iliad* is on the Greek side, but barely so. The parting of Hector and Andromache—a Trojan couple—under the menace of war, is one of the most affecting passages in the poem; and the culmination of the whole epic is the scene where Achilles and Priam—the best fighter of the Greeks and the king of Troy—sit down and weep together for what the war has cost them, the best friend of one and the son of the other.[12]

Those who want to enlist Faulkner as their propagandist usually ignore his frequent refusal to be one. Two examples will suffice here. Much has been made of the account in *Intruder in the Dust* of Chick Mallison's remembering Lucas just after Molly's death and "thinking with a kind of amazement: *He was grieving. You dont have to not be a nigger in order to grieve.*" This is plain and eloquent, and needs no comment. But an ignored passage later in the novel does. This same Chick Mallison, watching old Nub Gowrie confronting the sheriff over the grave he is about to open, "thought suddenly with amazement: *Why he's grieving*: thinking how he had seen grief twice now in two years where he had not expected it or anyway anticipated it, where in a sense a heart capable of breaking had no business being: once in an old nigger who had just happened to outlive his old nigger wife and now in a violent foulmouthed godless old man who had happened to lose one of [his] six lazy idle violent more or less lawless and a good deal more than just more or less worthless sons." [13] Faulkner underlines the parallel by italicizing the parallel phrases about grieving, and he himself points out the similarity of the two situations. But many of our critics who wax very emotional over the Negro flatly refuse, in spite of Faulkner's determined effort

---

[12]Homer, *Iliad*, VI, 390–493, and XXIV, 468–691.
[13]*Intruder in the Dust*, 25, 161.

to show both sides of the coin, to extend any sympathy or recognition to the grief of the white redneck.

A similar extended parallel is found in *Light in August*, in what is frequently called the "conditioning" of Joe Christmas. It is often maintained (though Faulkner expressly denies it) that Joe is a mere automaton whose history explains his character, and is consequently not morally responsible for his acts. But it is significant that when Faulkner introduces Percy Grimm, with his storm-trooper mentality, he gives a short history of his "conditioning" too. The intent here is perfectly clear. One may think what he will about predestination and free will, or any of the other names under which the same controversy is presented, but Faulkner makes it impossible for anyone to exonerate Joe Christmas and condemn Percy Grimm except by a flagrant act of intellectual dishonesty. They are equally innocent or equally guilty. Personally, I do not think that Faulkner, here or elsewhere, releases anyone from the burden of moral responsibility. But the point for us at this time is that he plays fair and shows no favoritism among his characters. He has the same breadth of view that has led generations of critics to apply the adjective *Olympian* to Goethe.

Coleridge said that one of the characteristics that distinguish the plays of Shakespeare from those of most other dramatists is his habit of "keeping at all times in the high road of life." He explains this phrase by saying that "Shakespeare has no innocent adulteries, no interesting incests, no virtuous vices;—he never renders that amiable which religion and nature alike teach us to detest, or clothes impurity in the garb of virtue . . . . Shakespeare's fathers are roused by ingratitude, his husbands stung by unfaithfulness; in him, in short, the affections are wounded in those points in which all may, nay, must, feel." [14] This applies almost equally well to Faulkner, who also stays with

---

[14]Samuel Coleridge, *Complete Works*, ed. Shedd (New York, 1884), IV, 62.

universally accepted human observations and values. He does not try to titillate us with the cute little tricks of an O. Henry or Maupassant, or with improbable sentimentalities like Bret Harte's villains with hearts of gold. Nor does he go overboard on the sentimentalities of his own time. Coleridge's point is entirely valid, though his language might put off some modern readers. The same essential observation has been made by modern critics who have commented that Faulkner "knew the human heart is the same in all latitudes and all epochs," [15] or have observed that in *Absalom, Absalom!* "the action represents issues of timeless moral significance." [16]

Two other ingredients of Faulkner's universality are too large for any but the most cursory treatment. These are the two which have given rise to much untenable mythic criticism and forced searching for literary influences simply because the evidence has been turned around. Both Faulkner's characters and his situations and conflicts bear the stamp of universal human experience, and hence it inevitably follows that close parallels will be found in the world's great literature and in mankind's fundamental myths. In illustrating this point briefly, I must emphasize that I am not assuming that Faulkner drew on or borrowed from the earlier myths or works, though it is entirely possible that in individual cases he may have done so.

Faulkner's characters, though sharply individualized, are very largely recognizable types. If people are truly drawn, this will inevitably happen, since (in spite of our current sentimentality about not categorizing people) people do tend to fall into such categories. A few examples will make the point clear. Dilsey is a highly individualized character, clearly of her own place and

---

[15] Maurice Edgar Coindreau, *The Time of William Faulkner: A French View of Modern American Fiction*, ed. and trans. by George McMillan Reeves (Columbia: University of South Carolina Press, 1971), 105.
[16] Ilse Dusoir Lind, "The Design and Meaning of *Absalom, Absalom!*," *PMLA*, 70 (1955), 887.

time. But she is also the eternal old female family servant, found in all ages and times where society has sufficient differentiation to create servants. I once did a study showing her basic relationship to David Copperfield's Peggoty, to Flaubert's Félicité, to Juliet's nurse, and on back through various other examples to medieval Japan in Lady Murasaki's *Tale of Genji*, and finally clear back to Odysseus' old nurse, Eurycleia—the only person in Ithaca who recognized him, on his return, by her own knowledge.[17] But Dilsey is not a stock character. She is an archetypal one. Stock characters are passed on from book to book—or from ad to ad—without touching life. They are things like the stage Irishman, or the southern girl or sheriff of TV commercials. Archetypal ones are drawn from life, but are real because life is both real and, in some respects, repetitious. Both Don Quixote and Emma Bovary are governed by an inability to distinguish fiction from fact. Don Quixote mistakes the myth of chivalry for the way the workaday world operates, as both Hightower and the Sartoris clan (in very different ways) try to live in the Civil War myth. Madame Bovary thinks that the world is, or should be, a romantic novel. The tall convict of *The Wild Palms*, who naïvely tries to rob a train as it is done in dime novels, is an archetypal brother to both the Don and Emma Bovary, as well as many another such deluded dreamer in both life and fiction.

Chick Mallison and Aleck Sander, like young Bayard and Ringo, are the perennial young leader and faithful friend and follower, corresponding to Gilgamesh and Engidu in the Babylonian epic, David and Jonathan, Achilles and Patroklus, Aeneas and Achates, Roland and Oliver, and a long line of other pairs in myth, history, and literature. Both the two types of characters and their relationship are universal, and conse-

---

[17]"Dilsey: From Faulkner to Homer," in *William Faulkner: Prevailing Verities and World Literature*, ed. Wolodymyr T. Zyla and Wendell M. Aycock (Proceedings of the Comparative Literature Symposium), VI (Lubbock: Texas Tech University, 1973), 57–75.

quently of interest to all areas and ages. Similarly, Sutpen is an Alexander the Great, a Julius Caesar, a Napoleon, a Hitler —with a strong dash of Faust, too.

The universal themes and situations that Coleridge mentioned are the basic elements of the world's myths and literature simply because they are basic to the human situation. Eula Varner's marriage to Flem Snopes is the universal theme of beauty and the beast. When Colonel Sartoris decides to go to town unarmed, knowing that it will cost him his life, he exactly parallels Goethe's Faust, who, just before his death, renounces magic and refuses to use it to defend himself against Care. And both the colonel and Faust are, in effect, reenacting Christ's refusal to respond to the taunt "If thou be the Son of God, come down from the cross." [18]

The theme of the idiot who is, in at least some respects, both wiser and more humane than those of normal intelligence appears in both Benjy, in *The Sound and the Fury*, and Ike Snopes, in *The Hamlet*. It is an ancient theme of both folklore and religion—note the concept of the "fool of Christ," and the fact that, etymologically, *cretin* is a form of *Christian*—and its most extended and sophisticated literary development is found in Dostoevsky's *The Idiot*.

The same dramatic encounter occurs in the confrontation between the old general and the corporal in *A Fable*, in Heinrich von Kleist's fine play *The Prince of Homburg*, and in Melville's *Billy Budd*. In all three cases the point is that a condemnation will be meaningless unless the condemned can be brought to accept its justice. It is closely related to the point made by the governor in *Requiem for a Nun*, when he refuses to pardon Nancy: "Who am I, to render null and abrogate the purchase she made with that poor crazed lost and worthless life?" [19]

---

[18]Matthew, 127:40.
[19]*Requiem for a Nun*, 210.

165

The conversion of a villain to a hero because of his suffering and sheer tenacity is a striking case of even-handed justice in the characters of Hagen (in the *Nibelungenlied*), Shakespeare's King Lear, and Faulkner's Mink Snopes.

This character brings up the last of my brief selection of universal themes. At the end of Mink's life we have an apotheosis of the common man, which is a striking example of a distinctively modern theme, treated also in two American poems—Edwin Arlington Robinson's "The Man Against the Sky" and Conrad Aiken's "Tetélestai." This theme gradually shades into an even grander and a much more ancient one: the ineffable vision of the glory and unity of the universe—the universal vision, in the most literal sense of the word. It is the theme of the mystics of all ages and religions, most tellingly presented (to me, at least) in the last canto of Dante's *Commedia*. But it is an equally effective secular theme, fully exploited, for example, in Ralph Hodgson's "The Song of Honor" and in a magnificent fifty-page passage in Hermann Broch's poem on the death of Vergil. And this is the apotheosis of Mink Snopes, a poor, mean, vicious sharecropper and murderer whose dying vision sees all the dead, "easy now, all mixed up comfortable and easy so wouldn't nobody even know or even care who was which any more, himself among them, equal to any, good as any, brave as any, being inextricable from, anonymous with all of them: the beautiful, the splendid, the proud and the brave, right on up to the very top itself among the shining phantoms and dreams which are the milestones of the long human recording—Helen and the bishops, the kings and unhomed angels, the scornful and graceless seraphim." [20]

---

[20]*The Mansion*, end of final sentence.

166

Contributors

MARGARET WALKER ALEXANDER was educated at Northwestern University and the University of Iowa. She has received a Yale Award for Younger Poets, fellowships from the Rosenwald and the Ford foundations, a Houghton-Mifflin Literary Fellowship, and a National Endowment for the Humanities fellowship. In addition, she has received honorary degrees from Denison University, Northwestern University, Rust College, and Morgan State University. Her famous novel *Jubilee* has been made into an opera, and the book itself is in its fortieth printing. Her works include *For My People, Prophets for a New Day, How I Wrote Jubilee, October Journey,* and, with Nikki Giovanni, *A Poetic Equation.* Ms. Alexander is presently at Jackson State University (Mississippi), where she is Professor of English and Director of the Institute for the Study of History, Life, and Culture of Black People.

CALVIN BROWN was a younger contemporary of William Faulkner in Oxford for many years. A graduate of the University of Mississippi, Mr. Brown went on to acquire degrees at the University of Cincinnati, Oxford University (first-class honors as a Rhodes Scholar), and the University of Wisconsin. His books include *Music and Literature, Repetition in Zola's Novels, Tones into Words,* and, most recently, *A Glossary of Faulkner's South.* Mr. Brown is Alumni Foundation Distinguished Professor of English and Comparative Literature at the University of Georgia.

Contributors

ALBERT J. GUERARD studied at Stanford and Harvard Universities and later taught at each. He has been a Fulbright fellow and has received fellowships from the Guggenheim, Ford, and Rockefeller foundations as well as from the National Foundation for the Arts and the National Foundation for the Humanities. He has received the *Paris Review* Fiction Prize and is a member of the American Academy of Arts and Sciences. In addition to six novels, he has written studies of the works of many other authors, including *Robert Bridges, Joseph Conrad, Thomas Hardy, Andre Gide*, and, most recently, *The Triumph of the Novel*, in which he examines the work of Dickens, Dostoevsky, and Faulkner. He is presently at Stanford University, where he is Albert L. Guerard Professor of Literature.

ILSE DUSOIR LIND, Professor of English at New York University, has held Ford Foundation and American Philosophical Society fellowships and has been Fulbright Lecturer in American Literature in Oslo, Norway, and visiting professor at the University of Hawaii's Faulkner seminar. She has presented numerous papers and published several articles on Faulkner's works, including "The Teachable Faulkner," "The Design and Meaning of *Absalom, Absalom!*," "Faulkner's Various Relationships with Nature," and "Faulkner and Racism." In addition, she presented "The Faulkner Who Wrote *As I Lay Dying*," a television lecture for the CBS Sunrise Semester, and was the featured speaker on the Faulkner program for the NBS series, "Nothing But Biography." For several years Ms. Lind has chaired the Special Faulkner Session at the Modern Language Association national convention.

LEWIS P. SIMPSON was educated at the University of Texas, where he also taught. He has been a consultant for the senior fellowship program in American literature for the National Endowment for the Humanities, Lamar Lecturer in Southern Literature at Mercer University, a member of the Christian Gauss Award Committee for Phi Beta Kappa, and a Guggenheim fellow. For many years he has been coeditor of *The Southern Review*. His books include *The Federalist Literary Mind*; *The Man of Letters in New England and the South*; *The Dispossessed Garden: Pastoral and History in Southern Literature*; *The Poetry of Community: Essays on the Southern Sensibility of History and Literature*; and *The Possibilities of Order: Cleanth Brooks and His Work*. Mr. Simpson is advisory editor to *Studies in American Humor* and has been on the editorial board of *American Literature*. He is presently at Louisiana State University, where he is William A. Read Professor of English.